A Dream in the Clouds

A politically-neutral collection of poetry, prose, and art
inspired by the 2008 United States Presidential
Election

A Dream in the Clouds

ISBN: 0981988199
ISBN 13: 9780981988191

Published by Bobo Strategy
Email: info@BoboStrategy.com
Website: http://www.BoboStrategy.com

Bobo Strategy
2506 N Clark St. #287
Chicago, IL 60614

Printed in the United States

Cover art by Nancie King Mertz – from "Sundown at Lincoln Memorial"

Table of Contents

Nancie King Mertz

Studio: 2936 N Clark, Chicago, IL - open daily.

Nancie has owned Artful Framer Studios, a custom framing firm, since 1979. In April 2009, Nancie received the "Distinguished Alumni" Award from the Graduate School at Eastern Illinois University. Nancie was named "Business Person of the Year 2008" by the Lincoln Park Chamber of Commerce; she was the "Artist of the Month" in <u>Artists' Magazine</u> and <u>Pastel Journal</u> in Sept. 2008, and "Official Artist of the Chicago Convention & Tourism Bureau" for 2005-2006 & 2006-2007. Artful Framer Studios was named "Small Business of the Year 2000" by Chicago's Lincoln Park Chamber of Commerce. She has served on several boards, including 13 years on the board of the Palette & Chisel Academy of Fine Arts, and is a strong supporter of philanthropic organizations in Chicago. She was appointed in Fall of 2008 to the Advocate Charitable Council. In 1999, Nancie was awarded the "Entrepreneurial Achievement Award" by the Network of Women Entrepreneurs and was President in 2000. She is a member of Holy Covenant United Methodist, serving as their gallery curator for 12 years. She is a member of the Chicago Pastel Painters and Pastel Society of America with signature status for both, a member of Oil Painters of America, and the Chicago Plein Air Painters. She's a member of the Rosalind Franklin Cooperative Medical Arts Group and part of the Door County Invitational Plein Air Festival.

Mark Brazaitis

Mark Brazaitis is the author of <u>The River of Lost Voices: Stories from Guatemala</u>, winner of the 1998 Iowa Short Fiction Award, and <u>Steal My Heart</u>, a novel published in 2000 by Van Neste Books. His latest book of fiction, <u>An American Affair: Stories</u>, won the 2004 George Garrett Fiction Prize from Texas Review Press. He is also the author of <u>The Other Language: Poems</u>, winner of the 2008 ABZ Poetry Prize, which was published in May of 2009. He is a past recipient of a National Endowment for the Arts fellowship, and his stories, poems and essays have appeared in <u>Ploughshares</u>, <u>The Sun</u>, <u>Witness</u>, <u>Beloit Fiction Journal</u>, <u>Confrontation</u>, <u>Notre Dame Review</u>, <u>Poetry East</u>, <u>Shenandoah</u>, and other literary magazines. A former Peace Corps volunteer, he directs the Creative Writing Program at West Virginia University, where he is an associate professor of English.

For more, see:
http://english.wvu.edu/graduate_studies/the_m_f_a_

One Last Long Drive

The last of my good friends, Aaron Miller, died the day before the 2008 presidential election. This was, all things considered, a blessing. For a year-and-a-half, he'd fought an increasingly hopeless battle with bladder cancer, and, in his final days, he was desperate for his struggle to end. Besides, he would have hated the election results.

Aaron was a McCain man, as was my good friend Peter Foster, who died of a heart attack on the first day of the 2008 Republican convention. My other two good friends, Sam Mitchell and Fernando Sanchez, would also have voted for McCain if they had been alive. Sam died of complications from diabetes on the December day in 2000 when the Supreme Court ruled in favor of George W. Bush over Al Gore. Fernando—we called him Frank—was killed in a car accident while on vacation in New Mexico the day Barack Obama gave his 2004 keynote speech to the Democratic convention.

I know that in the years ahead a vote for John McCain may come to seem as backwards and cautious as a vote for Stephen Douglas in the 1860 election. But I see myself in John McCain. Like McCain, I'm an old soldier, although my sacrifice was miniscule compared to his. And like McCain, I'm old period—I'll turn seventy-three on New Year's eve. Lastly, like McCain, I have an old-fashioned reverence for the United States of America. I maintain in my heart a patriotism untainted by irony or shame.

But the America I knew as a young man, and even as a man in his prime, is not the country I know now. I voted for John McCain because I thought he might restore America to a place I recognized and wanted to live in.

We buried Aaron, who was 76-years-old, in the Shadow Hill cemetery on the north side of our hometown of Sherman, Ohio. The November day was unusually temperate, and I could imagine Al Gore standing under the nearby crabapple tree, wagging a finger at us and saying, "See? Global warming is even coming to eastern Ohio." Since I retired from the marketing department of Auto Plus, a manufacturer of aftermarket hoods, doors, and fenders, I have become something of a political junkie, spending long hours in front of the television with candidates past and present. They are not always the best company, but I prefer them to silence.

After the burial, we gathered at Aaron's sister's house, in a den with a gas fireplace and a TV half the size of the room. There were twelve mourners, the men in gray suits and somber ties and the women in severe brown or midnight blue dresses. Add up our ages and we came close to a millennium. Aaron's sister suggested we each tell a story about Aaron, so we did, and we had a few laughs at his expense and our own. I choked up several times. I missed him; I missed all my departed friends.

Later, food was served. Even later, bottles of wine were opened, and stories about Aaron gave way to stories about anyone, which, after more wine, gave way to jokes. The punch line to one—about the president-elect—was "darkie," and it produced the evening's loudest laughter. There was relief in the laughter, as if, given the election results, people might have wondered whether such humor would be allowed anymore.

On occasions past, I would have laughed with them—and I would have defended the joke as innocuous, albeit crude. But this time, for reasons I couldn't have explained, I said goodbye and slipped outside. In the frigid night, I stopped a few feet from my Cadillac, glowing under a streetlight. My car, although only five years old, felt like a relic, an indulgence from a different era, when bigger was always better. Even as I slid inside it, apprehending its enormity, I began to mourn it. I couldn't afford the gas anymore.

Even so, as I drove the five-and-three-quarters miles back to my cabin above Sky Lake, I decided to plan one last long drive. I would leave behind the blue state of Ohio, and the new world it voted to join, and drive into West Virginia and Kentucky, reliable red-state bastions of the old world. It would be a farewell tour—my farewell to the old America, the America John McCain and I loved.

I had another reason for wanting to visit Kentucky. Owensboro, a town close to its westernmost border, was where Cindy McIntosh, a woman I'd been engaged to before I left for the army, moved with her husband nearly five decades ago. I had her address, and I thought I would pay her a visit—to come calling, as it were, on my past, to see what might be left of it.

•

I am a planner; anything rushed or spontaneously decided unsettles me. This was one of several areas of incompatibility Sarajane cited when she asked me for a divorce twenty-six years ago. She had other complaints about me—my snoring, my insistence on having my T-shirts folded in a particular way, my life-long belief in the justness of the Vietnam War. I never remarried.

In the week after Aaron's funeral, I prepared for my trip, suspending delivery of the newspaper for the four days I imagined I might be gone, having my mail held, ensuring I had sufficient quantities of the high-blood pressure medicine I've been taking for the last decade. I tidied up around my cabin, which I had moved into after my divorce. I thought living in a cabin would give me a rough edge, attractive to women, interesting to men. I reaped no such windfall. Even more than two decades later, I often feel like I am camping in my own home.

My daughter, Heather, lives in Charleston, West Virginia, where she works in advertising sales at the bigger of the city's two newspapers. She sometimes puts in twelve-hour days and brings work home with her. She jokes about living a big-city lifestyle in a sleepy Southern capital. Occasionally, she'll ask me what I do with all my free time, a question that never fails to offend me with its implications of sloth and uselessness. "I'm keeping tabs on the election" has been my answer for the past two years.

Charleston is on my way, more or less, to the far outposts of Kentucky, and if my daughter discovers that I have been through town and have failed to visit her, she will be upset. But if I see her, I know she will ask me, with the pinched-faced seriousness she displayed even as a child, whether it's wise for me to be driving so far, especially in winter.

As I settle into my Cadillac, I am surprised to find John McCain in the passenger seat. I am aware he is an apparition born of my bereavement and loneliness. But the friendless can't be choosers. And there's no one I would rather share a ride with than John McCain—unless it's Cindy McIntosh circa 1953.

"Are you ready, friend?" I ask him and he nods and the two of us hit the road.

We talk about growing up in a military family, a background we have in common. Even if I know everything he tells me, having read all of his books, it's good to hear it from him.

After I knock twice on the door of my daughter's ranch-style house on the city's northern edge, Bill, her husband, answers. It isn't far past nine in the morning, although Bill's appearance makes it seem even earlier. (In his defense, it is a Saturday.) His thin black hair, its recession having left a rainbow-like arc of pale skin above his forehead, shoots up in various directions. He is wearing a T-shirt and jeans but no shoes or socks.

Bill is the editorial page editor of the *Charleston Gazette*, and my daughter is his third wife, a workplace dalliance having become something legal and binding—at least for the time being. They don't have children, although Heather, who will turn forty the day after Obama's inauguration, says they're still considering it. "What do you know," Bill says, betraying no surprise at seeing me. "It's the early bird. You must have caught a boatload of worms by now." He smiles, blinks several times, and steps aside to let me in.

"I'm sorry I didn't call," I say. Their house smells like cats; they have four.

"If you had," Bill says, "you would have discovered that Heather isn't here."

"Oh," I say, stopping my progress toward the living room. If Heather isn't home, I have no reason to be here. I suspect Bill and I are able to maintain a polite relationship because we spend so little time with one another.

"Come in, come in," Bill says, waving me forward. "I can at least fuel you up with some coffee, although maybe you've had your fill already."

"Coffee would be fine. Thank you."

I keep instant coffee in my house; it's what I'm used to. When the first Starbucks opened in Sherman, I avoided it for a long time. "Coffee," I told anyone who would listen, "is coffee. In a paper cup with a green insignia, it's only more expensive coffee." I had my first cup of Starbucks coffee on my last date, four years ago, the night of the final presidential debate. The woman—I have forgotten her name—didn't care to talk about politics, and after half an hour, all I cared about was getting home for closing statements.

From the kitchen, Bill tells me that Heather and several of her "single, divorced, and/or empty-nest-mother friends" rented a van and drove to Atlantic City.

"But Heather doesn't gamble," I say.

"Well, then she must be off having an affair," Bill says good-humoredly.

Bill brings me a cup of coffee. "It's Newman's Breakfast Blend," he says. "Paul Newman," he adds needlessly. "Don't worry, it isn't specially formulated to poison Republicans."

"Newman was a limousine liberal if ever there was one." I can't help provoking him.

"He was worse," Bill says, smiling. "He was a race-car liberal. Burned all that fossil fuel in cars going around and around an oval—the very definition of meaningless waste."

It's difficult to argue with Bill because he often undercuts his opinions with offbeat humor. I suppose this, too, is how we've managed to get along.

I know exactly where Bill stood in the election. He wrote the *Gazette's* endorsement of Obama. Heather, meanwhile, had been a strong supporter of Hillary Clinton and, in the general election, had threatened to vote for either Bob Barr or Ralph Nadar. "But don't worry, Dad," she told me, "I won't even tease you by saying I'll consider voting for McCain."

Bill and I discuss the election results. After he runs down Obama's potential cabinet, he asks me, "How are the fish biting?"

"The fish?" I say.

"Or the women."

"Well, I'd say the pond's stocked but the fisherman's sleeping in his rowboat."

Bill laughs more than my joke deserves, but I appreciate it.

There is a short silence. "I've been married three times, have I ever mentioned that?" he asks me.

He grins because his marital track record had been a point of contention with me before Heather married him. "I think I can tell you this now: Even after I married Heather, I didn't know if I had it in me to be a good husband, to be attentive and interested and, more important, to give a goddamn if the marriage succeeded or failed."

My initial reaction is to respond with something sarcastic and judgmental, something like, "You and Bill Clinton." But I understand this might stop our conversation.

"At a certain point," Bill says, "maybe around my forty-seventh birthday, which seemed a significant milestone somehow, maybe because it was the age my father was when he died, something shifted in me." Bill pats at his hair, a gesture that fails to corral its wild appearance. "I wasn't hungry for what I used to be hungry for, but for closeness, tenderness, warmth, the presence of someone I loved, who happened to be my wife. It was a strange and even frightening transformation. I'd gone from being afraid of caring too little to being afraid of being too needy, of being too vulnerable to losing her."

Bill smiles at me. It's a different smile than I've seen on him. It's soft, a little bemused. "I almost told her not to go on this trip," he says in a near whisper. "I almost said, 'I'll miss you too much.'"

"It's a new day," I tell Bill, which is all I can think to say. I remember what my ex-wife said once about my emotions, that they ranged from the basement to the attic of a house flattened by King Kong. If I ever felt what Bill is feeling, it was only when I was engaged to Cindy McIntosh.

"A new day," Bill repeats with enthusiasm.

"Right. A new day. A new president. And a new Bill Skidmore, who has come to realize he's madly, tragically, in love with his wife." There is a pause, and Bill smiles the old smile. "A wife who is off in Atlantic City, picking up Black Jack dealers and Chippendale dancers and partying until dawn." He smiles again, this time shy and vulnerable. "I've called her once this morning. Do you think it's too soon to call her again?" He holds up his hand. "I've got to be strong, I know. More coffee?"

I decline, although not without regret; Bill is obviously in the mood to talk, and I wouldn't mind getting to know my son-in-law better. At the front door, he reaches toward me, and it is a moment before I understand he is giving me a hug. My left hand does a tap dance on his back. On the awkwardness scale, our goodbye is a nine. I tell him I'm glad we had a chance to chat. For once, I mean it.

I soon find myself back in my Cadillac. McCain has waited for me. "Did I tell you about the first time I saw Cindy?" he asks.

"Cindy McIntosh?"

"My Cindy. Cindy McCain née Hensley, not the sweetheart you loved and lost." There is a pause; McCain smiles. "Fireworks. Lightning. All the bright and explosive clichés." McCain's smile fades, and he glances out the window. He wears a thoughtful look, with a hint of sorrow. It's a look he rarely showed the world during his mostly angry campaign. "I did something destructive after I met her, of course. I broke up my marriage, my family. Self-imposed change can be as rough as any."

I pull off for gas at the Flying J in Catlettsburg, Kentucky, right over the West Virginia line. The Flying J includes a stall of showers—a quarter buys a minute of hot water—and a cafeteria-style food service. I'm not hungry, but I figure if I eat now, I won't have to stop later. I want to get to Owensboro before dark—before dinner, if I can—and I'll save at least fifteen minutes by having lunch here instead of elsewhere on the road.

I order two pieces of fried chicken with sides of mashed potatoes and green beans, and I find a seat on a hard plastic chair near the entrance to the shower areas. I've had only minimal contact with truckers in my life, and I've lived with two opposing stereotypes of them. The first is of the trucker as romantic patriot, putting in ten- and twelve- and fourteen-hour days on the road, hopping on the CB occasionally for companionship but mostly living inside his head, thinking of the wife and children he left behind and the wide, wonderful country he's driving across. The second stereotype is of the trucker as lonesome and lecherous, holing up at truck stops to partake of teenage prostitutes or giving rides to hitchhikers in exchange, as the old bumper sticker had it, for "gas, grass, or ass" because "nobody rides for free."

A pair of truck drivers, both perhaps in their mid-forties, sit at the table across from me. I think they're talking about the election because I hear the word "change" twice. I have to believe they're McCain voters, men who cherish the America of broad plains and abide reluctantly the America of cramped and chaotic cities with their discordant medleys of foreign languages. Like me, they have been thrust into a strange new world.

After I've finished my meal and have stood to discard my chicken bones, I say to the two men, "Our new president will probably require you to drive wind-powered rigs. You'll be sailing down the highway at a maximum of 25 knots per hour. If you're lucky, you'll make it across the country in a month." I laugh at my joke.

The men glance up at me with uncomfortable smiles. From up close, I have a better look at them: The man nearest me sports a delicate mustache, thin blades of strawberry-blond hair, and on his forearm, peaking from beneath the right sleeve of his maroon sweater vest, is a tattoo of a butterfly. His lunch companion's left foot is sticking from beneath his table; he's wearing purple Converse All-Stars. There is a gold stud in his left ear.

Realizing I've likely misjudged who they are, I feel my lower lip tremble, my version of a blush. I know I should excuse myself and move on, but words leave my lips: "I met John McCain once, in a bowling alley in South Carolina." This isn't even true. It was Aaron Miller who met McCain in the Charleston, South Carolina, bowling alley during the 2000 primary, when George W. Bush was re-writing the book on dirty tricks with his racist phone campaign about McCain's adopted daughter. "We talked, believe it or not, about losing with dignity," I tell them. "Of course, he was referring to bowling."

I manufacture a smile, which the man with the purple sneakers returns. "It's good to have a sense of humor," he says.

I expect him to say more, but he doesn't, and I am happy to leave the scene after saying, "Safe travels."

I exit by a different door than I came in. To my left is a lineup of eight trucks, waiting for their drivers to return from their showers or lunch. I walk to the right, and I find my Cadillac tucked between a pair of SUVs as square as tanks. Both have McCain/Palin bumper stickers, and I consider waiting until one of the SUV's owners returns so I might have the kind of conversation I expected to have with the two men inside. But I remember my mission, and I slide into my Cadillac, turn the key, and resume my trip.

"If the presidency had come down to a bowling match," McCain tells me, "you might well have seen me in the White House."

"But can you bowl with your war injuries?"

He winces. "Hell, maybe I was doomed to lose no matter what the game." His grin is a combination of bravado and wistfulness. "But I think I might have come closer in bowling."

I tell him about my own physical shortcomings, about how I used to run at least three miles four times a week before the arthritis in my knees made even walking a battle sometimes. "And my night vision is terrible," I say. "Driving at night, I feel like I'm walking in a cave with only a birthday candle to light the way."

"If we're still driving at dusk, let me out and I'll hitchhike. Kentucky is crawling with wildlife. I don't want a deer flying through the windshield to share my seat." He laughs good-naturedly, and I join in. The needle hits seventy and I activate the cruise control.

"I might be losing a few battles with age," I tell McCain, "but I'm hoping for a drawn-out war. My mother was ninety-five when she died."

"My mother," he says, "is still alive."

It is late afternoon when I arrive in Owensboro. The sky is a somber gray thanks to a combination of clouds and the coming night. I have been following directions I printed off MapQuest. Relying on computerized driving directions is a recent failing. For years after I could have used Google or Yahoo—or invested in a global positioning system—I relied on old-fashioned maps, plotting my journeys, such as they were, on the kitchen table the night before I was to leave. I wonder if map reading will become an arcane skill, like glass blowing or writing poetry.

I exit the Wendell H. Ford Expressway, but because of the dim light, I cannot read my directions. On Frederica Street, I stop in front of the Blind Parrot Bar & Grill. I click on my overhead light. My directions appear indecipherable, like a code to which I've lost the key.

"You need to backtrack a little," McCain tells me. "A left turn becomes a right turn. Or, to reflect the will of the people, perhaps I should say a right turn becomes a left."

He's correct, and in less than ten minutes, I have pulled up to the curb in front of Cindy Synder née McIntosh's two-story, redbrick house, which features, as I suspected it might, a white picket fence. The fence, as I see upon stepping out of my Cadillac, isn't immaculate. The bottoms of most of the posts are sprinkled with mud, and there is a hole in the middle of three contiguous posts, as if a wild animal had crashed through. The grass could use cutting, although perhaps Cindy and her husband—Robert is his name—didn't anticipate having to do any mowing past October.

I walk up the concrete path and grip the knocker. This is your last chance to turn back, I tell myself, and I glance to the right, to the Ford Taurus in the open garage. I see a McCain sticker on the bumper, and my hand lifts the knocker high and gives three decisive thumps on the door.

Five seconds later, the door opens, and I am staring at someone who could be my brother. He is my height—an even six feet—and has the same thin, snow-white hair. His skin is wrinkled most noticeably around the eyes.

"John?" he asks, and I have the thrilling thought that he has mistaken me for McCain. But: "Oh. I thought you were my neighbor."

I introduce myself and tell him I've been traveling. "I remembered that Cindy McIntosh—your wife, I presume—moved here, and since I was in the neighborhood, so to speak, I thought I'd come by to say hello."

He looks at me carefully with his cloudy but penetrating dark eyes. "You wouldn't happen to be her ex-fiancé?"

His knowledge of this fact astonishes me, and I don't know what to say. I decide, eventually, on the truth: "Yes."

"Well, come on in."

He leads me to a living room with a pair of couches facing each other across a coffee table. From one couch, he slides a pile of clothes—I notice a pair of red-white-and-blue Jockey shorts—onto the floor. "Have a seat," he says. "Drink?"

"Water would be fine," I say.

"I'm better supplied than that," he says. But despite the Taurus's bumper sticker, I don't know in whose territory I am in, friend or foe, and I decide against alcohol. "Water would be fine," I repeat.

He returns with a glass of tap water, no ice, a shot glass, and a fifth of Jack Daniel's. I notice an encrusted red streak on the side of my glass, as if whoever last handled it first stuck his fingers in spaghetti sauce. The water tastes faintly of iron.

He and I sit on opposite couches, and he looks me over carefully before saying, "The only way Cindy could have found two more similar looking men was if she had gone to a convention of twins."

He is right, of course, so I smile. "And at the end," he continues, "she said we were dead alike in another way—we were married to routine. Cindy said we were born nostalgic, bemoaning the lost paradise of the womb."

"I'm sorry," I say. I hadn't counted on having another person I'd loved, albeit long ago, to mourn.

He cocks his head to the right. "Sorry about what?"

"I'm sorry about the loss of...I'm sorry Cindy died."

After a pause, he smiles. "Died?" He laughs, two sharp bursts of sound. "If only! She didn't die—she flew! Back in 1968, she decided she was going to volunteer in the Eugene McCarthy for President campaign. She never came back. For the last, I don't know, forty years, she's been living in San Francisco, running a battered women's shelter and painting murals of rainbows and street musicians."

"San Francisco," I say in the way I might pronounce a foreign phrase.

"The capital of the Left Coast," he says.

"San Francisco," I repeat. It still doesn't sound right on my tongue.

"You'll have a drink now, I bet," he says, lifting the bottle of Jack Daniel's. No small part of me is tempted. But I can see drinking myself into an overnight stay at Robert's house and waking the next morning feeling like I was in a car wreck. "No, I better push off," I say.

"Right," he says. "Bon voyage." He fills his shot glass again and downs it before standing to see me to the door.

Before I step outside, I turn to him and say, "How did you know who I was?"

Robert shakes his head. "It wasn't me who knew. It was Cindy. I spoke with her a day or two before the election—she checks in every six months or so to see if I'm still breathing—and she said, 'If John McCain doesn't win, I wouldn't be surprised if one of us hears from an ex-soldier, ex-fiancé of mine who's looking to find the past.'" He pauses. "Apparently you'd written her a letter, which I must have forwarded, after the first presidential debate. She said you had seen the future and you were sad to report it wasn't John McCain."

"I forgot about that," I say.

"You'd also dropped her a line after Richard Nixon died."

I sigh. "I loved Nixon."

"You'll hear no argument from me." Robert rubs his forehead. "And after Gerald Ford passed on, you..."

"Right," I say. "She never wrote back."

"I don't have to tell you how hard-hearted she can be," Robert says. "She's also one busy lady. Listen, are you sure you don't want to stay? I can make a pot of coffee and we can watch a couple of Ronald Reagan movies I have on tape."

The offer is tempting—I haven't seen *Bedtime for Bonzo* since the week of Reagan's death—but I have the feeling I would feel no better in the morning.

"I appreciate it," I say. "I do." And I am about to tell him about having McCain in my car, but he would either think I'm crazy or want to join me. I say goodbye.

In my Cadillac again, I drift out of town. McCain and I don't speak for a while. At last, I say, "Cindy and I dated for four-and-a-half months and got engaged the day before I shipped off to Germany. We exchanged letters, at first once a day, then once a week. Eventually, she wrote to tell me she'd met a man from Owensboro, Kentucky—a man, come to think of it now, who reminded her of me—and couldn't keep her promise."

"Heartbreaking," McCain says.

"It was," I concede. "My life was going to be perfect with Cindy McIntosh, and every woman I met thereafter fell short of her standard. But I guess I didn't know who Cindy McIntosh was. I suppose she didn't either." I glance at McCain, who looks distracted.

Perhaps he, too, is looking back, thinking about what his presidential campaign might have been, although I doubt a different formula—a different running mate, a more consistent message, an operatic humming of "Anchors Away" during the third presidential debate—would have altered the outcome.

"I should probably confess to you that I wasn't much of a soldier," I tell him. "I've even told a few people that I served in Vietnam when I actually spent my entire two-year military career in Munich. The closest I've ever come to Vietnam is watching *Apocalypse Now*, and I had to leave the theater after the first hour. My stomach couldn't take it."

McCain looks at me. I've always thought of him as a handsome man, especially with his cool, luminous eyes. But age has crept in everywhere on his face, turning it into a cracking stone. "We all have parts of our past we aren't proud of," he says. He pauses, looks at me, looks out his window. "I don't have to tell you I didn't run the most elegant campaign."

"You did what you thought you had to do."

"I could have done better. I wish I had."

Minutes pass. "Where are we going?" he asks.

"I guess I'm looking for a hotel."

"Drive much farther and we'll be spending the night in a state won by my opponent." He sounds disapproving. Or is he only resigned? "But go on—be part of tomorrow."

"I don't think I'll ever be part of tomorrow."

"Don't sell yourself short," he says, his voice less heavy. "I bet you're looking at another decade on this planet, at least."

I never thought I would outlive all my friends, be the last man standing, albeit with a crick in my back. What will I do for company now? The election is over. "Maybe I'll keep driving all the way to San Francisco," I say. "Show up on Cindy McIntosh's doorstep in a Greenpeace T-shirt and a Che Guevara beret."

"I like that attitude. I'd call you a maverick if I wasn't sick of the word." McCain smiles, and I am about to tell him how good it is to have his company when, as if born from the night air, there is a sixteen-point buck standing no more than twenty yards in front of me. Swiftly, I turn the Cadillac's wheel to the left, but I am sure the buck will startle and move directly in front of me. I prepare for the impact, for a shattered windshield, for pain.

But the buck, as if it is a front lawn Christmas ornament—one of Santa's bulkier reindeer—or the reincarnated spirit of a Buddhist monk, stands dead still. It doesn't move as my Cadillac, at sixty-five-miles-per-hour, slides past it, with no more than a foot between us. Indeed, the buck is so close, and so large, I have the feeling it is sitting in the passenger seat with McCain.

A moment later, I have driven well past it, and when I look in my rearview mirror, I cannot see it anywhere. My heart is thundering against my chest, and I feel I might choke on my adrenaline. Why didn't I die? I ask myself.

I slow down. Sixty-five becomes fifty-five becomes fifty.

"Damn," I say. "How did I make it? How the hell did I make it out alive?"

"It's a sign," McCain says.

"Of what?" I ask.

"I think you know."

In the headlight's glare, a sign welcomes us to Illinois. "We're in a blue state," I say, and I'm sure my giddy tone is due to the collision I avoided, the catastrophe I averted, rather than a new hopefulness about my country or my place in it.

But thinking McCain might misinterpret it, I turn to him to explain. He's gone.

I look again in my rearview mirror. I see only the night I've driven though.

Bill Brown

A part time lecturer at Vanderbilt University, Bill Brown is the author of four collections of poetry, three chapbooks and a textbook. His latest book of poems was released in 2008 from Iris Press. The recipient of many fellowships and awards, his recent work appears in <u>Tar River Poetry</u>, <u>Southern Poetry Review</u>, <u>Prairie Schooner</u>, <u>North American Review</u>, <u>Rattle</u>, <u>Texas Poetry Review</u> and <u>Connecticut Review</u>.

Landscape, West Tennessee, 1962

West Tennessee schools closed for cotton picking,
so Finley and Hog Wallow kids could drag burlap bags

behind them like bad memories—stuffed with middling,
sharp hulls and sweat. The September scorch burnt

white necks red and browned arms and hands.
Most pickers were Negroes from the bottoms,

glad to have enough work to survive part of a year.
Back in school, pigeons outside Latin class

cooed their morning prayers. Miss Kirby closed
the windows to keep out the heat. We simmered

in stale air and boredom. Becky Lewis sat in back,
her cheerleader skirt hiked and I learned nothing.

Fall maples turned red. The blue sky was blank.
At first freeze we went rabbit hunting. We walked

stubbled cotton fields with pocks of mud and ice
to startle rabbits from their hiding. Talk of civil rights

sandwiched our little town. Birds of a feather my uncle preached.
In spring pigeons outside Latin class cooed their morning prayers.

Miss Kirby closed the window to keep out the cool.
We simmered in stale air and boredom. Who would

guess a black man would one day be our President,
the year Becky Lewis sat in back and I learned nothing.

Lauren Camp

Lauren Camp (Santa Fe, New Mexico) is an artist and educator, working in a confluence of visual, musical and literary arts. Her first book of poems will be published by West End Press in 2010. Her website is http://www.laurencamp.com

Inauguration

We have emerged into the glint
of cold sunlight, calling only one name
from hurricane to quiet field,
from a great gash of red stripes
to a village of people swooping and singing,
building the wings of this universe
out of bending bones of history.

On this day of putting things right,
the day reason smooths into promise,
I am proud of my country,
upthrust with light.

When Senator Feinstein says
United States of America,
each gilded word somersaults off her tongue,
flipping and jumping into the air,
into the big world of thieves and saints,
teasing into the ears of other countries
and returning with their stories.
Listening, I am able to release and forgive;
the *still waters of peace** wash over me.

Yes, we are at the bottom
of the ferris wheel, but finally looking up
into the thick blue sky
with Dr. King on the seat next to us,
touching his strong face toward heaven,
freedom words tumbling dark
and able-bodied from his mouth

like expanding light through clouds
into the ears of his blessed congregation.

And the burning gospel of history
rolls forth from Aretha's throat
becoming a slow dirt of blues, wringing
trust from anthems, her voice
ringing with pride.

We have begun rewriting the future
of the shattered world.
The long slow sound of ancient music
waves through the people
who stream like a banner on the lawn.

*The "still waters of peace" comes from President Barack Obama's Inaugural
Address, January 20, 2009: "Forty-four Americans have now taken the presidential
oath. The words have been spoken during rising tides of prosperity and the still
waters of peace."

Nini Castañeda

Nini was born in Bogota, Colombia on a Monday morning in September 1982. She obtained her bachelor's degree (with honors) in Visual Arts at the Javeriana University of Bogotá, Columbia in 2005.

Looking for more knowledge in the area of film, she came to Paris to study a MFA in Filmmaking at The International Film School of Paris (2008). She recently finished her first film <u>Sugar Rush</u> (2008), and she has continued working on her illustrations, which she started back in Colombia.

She currently lives in Paris and can be reached by email at: <u>yoninita@gmail.com</u>

Barbara Crooker

Despite being the full-time caregiver of a child with autism (who is still at home), Barbara Crooker has published over 650 poems in over 1975 publications, including magazines such as Yankee, The Christian Science Monitor, The Beloit Poetry Journal, The Christian Century, River City, America, The Atlanta Review, Green Mountains Review, and The Denver Quarterly; anthologies, including The Bedford Introduction to Literature and The Bedford Introduction to Poetry, Good Poems for Hard Times (Garrison Keillor, editor)(Viking Penguin), Sweeping Beauty: Contemporary Women Poets Do Housework, (University of Iowa); ten chapbooks, and three full-length books, Radiance, which won the 2005 Word Press First Book Award and was a finalist for the 2006 Paterson Poetry Prize; Line Dance (Word Press, 2008), which won the 2009 Paterson Prize for Literary Excellence; and More, which is forthcoming from C & R Press in 2010. She has received three Pennsylvania Council on the Arts Fellowships in Literature, twenty-six Pushcart Prize nominations, thirteen residencies at the Virginia Center for Creative Arts, was a finalist for a Grammy Award (Spoken Word Category), and won these national poetry competitions: the 1997 Karamu Poetry Prize, the New Millennium Writings Y2K Award, the 2001 ByLine Chapbook Competition, the 2003 Thomas Merton Poetry of the Sacred Award, the 2004 WB Yeats Society of NY Poetry Prize, the 2004 Grayson Books Chapbook Competition, The 2006 Rosebud Ekphractic Poetry Prize, and 2007 the Pen and Brush Poetry Prize. Garrison Keillor has read seventeen of her poems on The Writer's Almanac.

The Morning After

So I run into Sam, in the grocery store, knowing she'd run for Congress but lost, and I'm thinking uh-oh, this is going to be awkward, as I give her a hug, because her opponent ran a nasty campaign, and I think about all the long boring hours we've just put in: doors slammed in our faces, phones slammed in our ears, data entered late at night as my contact lenses turned to sandpaper; but also the good stuff: a group of black kids standing on a street corner with signs saying "Honk if you love Obama" and then a fire truck came by who *really* made some noise; the middle-aged women I phone-banked with who elbowed each other out to take pictures with their Iphones of them next to a cardboard cutout of the man; the elderly and disabled I drove to the polls who wanted to cast their ballots in person even though it was hard; my four-year old grandson who said, awestruck, over every African-American man over twenty that he saw in the last six months, "Oh, look; it's Bawack Obama;" and Sam hugs me back with a smile bright as the sun coming up over South Mountain, and says, "It's a *great* day to be a Democrat!"

Grace Atuhaire

Grace Atuhaire, born in 1988. A member of Uganda Women Writers Association (FEMRITE) in Uganda, she writes poetry for all age groups and teaches poetry at the Bavubuka foundation in Uganda. Her poem "home" was published in a FEMRITE anthology: Farming Ashes.

Who says God is not black?

At the well
Every one screams Obama!
Who is Obama?

The kikuyu say he is ours!
The Americans say he is ours!

While I sleep
My wife whispers Obama!
Who is Obama?

'He is the truth' for Kenya
He is light for America
He is the way for the world

Paul Hodges

Paul Hodges is a writer, actor, and storyteller. Dozens of his poems, essays, and stories have been included in various magazines and anthologies, including several chapters from his memoir, <u>Little House on Miller Road: Growing Up in the Real Mayberry</u>. A cum laude graduate of Duke University, he is coordinator for the Mount Airy Downtown Business Association, and an odd-job handyman. He has performed his three one-man shows, on Bobby Kennedy, Edgar Allan Poe, and William Shakespeare at various venues, including the public schools. A member of *Imagine That! Storytelling Guild*, he has performed at various venues, including the annual *Tellabration!* event. His philosophy, boiled down to its essence: Do not be mean.

The Inauguration of Barack Obama

I saw a man by the side of the road –
A plain-looking man, an ordinary-seeming man,
A man of means and modesty, a white man –
Walking his dog, waving the American flag.

I heard a woman at a check-out counter –
A normal woman, a working woman,
A woman of years and tears, a white woman –
Proclaim this to be the day she'd been waiting for.

I smelled hope and promise in the air.
I tasted victory and redemption
I felt truly a part of the American community,
Happy to be a citizen, proud to be a patriot.

The commons of the country, the Washington Mall,
Mirrored the mosaic that is the United States
Short, tall, fat, skinny, young, old,
Bearded, freshly-shaved, long hair, short hair,
Rich, poor, strong, weak, nondescript, beautiful:

All enthralled by the majesty of the moment,
All enlivened by hope long deferred,
Bound together by promise achieved,
Celebrating in harmony and peace.

Paul Hostovsky

Paul Hostovsky's poems appear widely online and in print. He has been featured on Poetry Daily, Verse Daily, The Writer's Almanac, and Best of the Net. His poems have won a Pushcart Prize, the Muriel Craft Bailey Award from The Comstock Review, and chapbook contests from Grayson Books, Riverstone Press, Frank Cat Press, and Split Oak Press. He has two full-length collections, Bending the Notes (2008), and Dear Truth (2009), both available from Main Street Rag. To read more of Paul's poetry, visit his website at: http://www.paulhostovsky.com

Lessons on Election Day

On Tuesday we might
dissect a squid.
A squid is an invertebrate.
It's squishy and has
an outer protective shell
called an exoskeleton.
It has a mantle and a jet
propulsion.
It's a mollusk.
Mollusk is a phylum.
There are lots of species
in a phylum
but there are only 8 phyla
in the whole thing,
and California has the most
popular people
because they're worth
55 electoral votes,
and to be the President
you have to be born
in America,
and you have to go
to an electoral college,
and you have to have
a spine.

Ben Humphrey

Ben Humphrey is a Retired Professor of Pediatric Oncology (M.D., Ph.D. from the University of Chicago). He now lives at 9,300 feet in the Rocky Mountains. He has been writing poetry since 2003 and has published in both American and European literary journals. Ben is an active member of Poetry West (associate with Colorado College in Colorado Springs) and has served on its Board of Directors.

Call for a Third *Corps of Discovery*

1948, "I will never live to see
a Negro in the oval office"
my father said. Black and Afro American
were not used as labels when I was a boy.

2008, progress! Now I may never live to see
a Ms President, trusted for a long journey
into a world weary wilderness,
another Sacagawea to lead the way.

Were You There When the High Price Was Paid?

"They are very poor down there"
my dad said in a pensive voice
that got my attention.
He'd been down South.

"Homes are shacks, a hand pump in the front yard,
food comes from a garden, chickens,
a pig or two. They buy as little as possible
from the general store

where a pack of twenty cigarettes
cost twenty cents for those with money.
From an open pack in a mason jar
the poor can buy two for a nickel."

An ominous tale for an eight year old,
an allegory for later years.
Too young to fully understand
but old enough to remember

when the TV screen projected the pain,
canines, clubs, bodies dragged to jail,
others dredged from rivers and ponds,
a shallow grave for three in a gravel pit.
Stark images, reawakened
of that voter registration
when the highest price was paid
for success in two thousand and eight.

- for James Earl Chaney, murdered June 21, 1964

51

Allison Joseph

Allison Joseph lives, writes and teaches in Carbondale, Illinois, where she directs the MFA Program in Creative Writing at Southern Illinois University Carbondale. She also serves as editor and poetry editor of <u>Crab Orchard Review</u>, a national journal of literary works, and director of the Young Writers Workshop, a coed residential creative writing summer workshop for high-school aged writers.

The Night the Poets Watched Palin

the women in the room grew particularly pissed,
so angry at how she'd mangle the English
we'd all spent years charming and seducing,
we watched the debate's first half
with the sound turned off, sinking in our fury

into the luxurious leather decadence
of Chad and Gwen's living room set.
Perhaps she reminded us all of the schoolmarm
pint-sized versions of Van Halen lusted after
in the immortal "Hot for Teacher" video,

chick who pulls off classroom garb
to reveal her inner bathing suit,
beauty queen sash snug around persuasive hips
as she thrashed before middle school charges.
When we did turn the sound up,

pure malice poured among us as easily
as wine, disbelief too--"Did she just wink
at us?" and "No she didn't just say "shout-out"
in a vice-presidential debate"--bewilderment
that hushed pundit voices praised her afterwards.

Maybe she brought back that girl we'd all known
in high school, nymphet male teachers desired
despite all statutes to the contrary,
tottering into class in stilettos and Jordache jeans,

Love's Baby Soft drifting off her shoulders

like incense, or the girl who sits
in the back of our classes now,
not answering any question you pose
on any book you've assigned,
preferring to ask you instead

why we needed to read it at all, cell phone
an insolent charm she dangles from her wrist,
ready to text as soon as you dismiss class
and she dismisses you, darting where pretty girls
congregate not to read or write, or do calculus.

C. F. Kelly

Cornelius F. Kelly began writing poetry seriously in 1995. He has published in a variety of newspapers and magazines including <u>Pinedale Roundup</u>, <u>American Cowboy</u>, <u>AIM Magazine</u>, <u>Streetviews</u>, and <u>Wyoming Magazine</u>. As Lugnaquilla Press, he has published eight chapbooks: <u>Pinedale Poems</u>, <u>People Poems</u>, <u>Haiku</u>, <u>Copos de Nieve</u> (Spanish), <u>Letters from Mae</u> (a collection of his mother's letters from 1921 to 1936), <u>Paint Pots</u> (a collection of children's poetry), <u>Poetry for Poets</u>, and <u>Poetry Laugh Lines</u>. He has published in <u>Haiku Quarterly</u> of Swindon, England, and done readings of his Spanish Poetry in Managua, Nicaragua, and in Granada, Spain. He is a septuagenarian who says that writing poetry directs his focus, clarifies his thought, and shapes his language. It makes the ordinary special, gives beauty to the common, and elevates the soul. He is an active member of WYOPoets and of Wyoming Writers, Inc. His neglected web page is: http://myweb.wyoming.com/~ckelly/default.htm

Grandmothers

Mama Sarah's house in Kenya
has a tin roof that provides
rain music in monsoon
and sun shade in summer.

She and Oyango and his other wives
live in Kogelo, and she and Akumu—
wife number one—welcome the birth
in 1936 of Barack Hussein Obama.

They help him pack for the journey
to Hawaii and wave good-bye
as the local bus departs loudly
on the dusty track to Nairobi.

There on the island, a grandson is born
who continues the Obama name
who is a United States citizen by birth
who has the potential to become President.

Mama Sarah rocks in reverie recalling
the Mau Mau-British independence struggles
the imprisonment of Jomo Kenyatta
and his ultimate presidency of her country.

She shudders as the Luo and the Kikuyu
match machetes in the streets over
a disputed election and ancient rivalries
in destructive conflicts needing resolution.

She rocks and waits patiently to see
if the young Barack will succeed
with his lofty aspirations in a land
so distant, so foreign, and so powerful.

Susanna Lang

Susanna Lang's collection of poems, <u>Even Now</u>, was published in 2008 by <u>The Backwaters Press</u>. More recently, her poem "Condemned" won the Inkwell competition, judged by Major Jackson. Her poems have appeared or are forthcoming in journals including <u>New Letters</u>, <u>The Sow's Ear Poetry Review</u>, <u>The Baltimore Review</u>, <u>Kalliope</u>, <u>Green Mountains Review</u>, <u>Jubilat</u>, and <u>Rhino</u>. Translations include <u>Words in Stone</u> and <u>The Origin of Language</u>, both by Yves Bonnefoy. A poem published in <u>The Spoon River Poetry Review</u> won a 1999 Illinois Arts Council award. She has lived in Chicago for 32 years, and works for the Chicago Public Schools.

After the Election

Atlanta, December 23, 2008

The signs—
          VOTE EARLY!
still stand in the yards
nearly two months later
decked with Christmas lights.

Up in Chicago we say
Vote early and often.
Part of the ritual,
like mistletoe.

                    *

Atlanta, December 26, 2008

At the foot of the neighbor's driveway

Christmas wrappings bundled for recycling;
a dribble of plastic soldiers
no more than two inches high;

last year's Christmas lights, discarded
because no one could figure out which bulb
was making the whole string blink;

and prickly balls that fell from the sweetgum tree—
the old cleared out to make way for the new.

*

Sweetwater Creek, January 1, 2009

Sweetgum trees by the creek, and the stones
laid so sweet, one on the other,
that the retaining wall leading to the millrace
still stands, though it was built before
the Civil War; built by slaves, the mill itself
still black from Sherman's fire.

*

East Chicago, November 3, 2008

When I was a child, the Fuller Brush man
came to the door, and my mother
stood in the doorway to buy his brushes.

Here in this half-abandoned town where the mills
are dark and silent, our knock
echoes down the stairs, and a woman calls to walk
        on in.

She is washing dishes at the sink.
A man says, *Don't forget to go next door.*
A young man says, *Voting for the other guy.*
        And laughs.

They know where to find their polling place,
they know what the hours are, but
they still want the doorhanger.

        *

Grant Park, November 4, 2008

Then we were all there, in the park
        with the cut-out buildings
etched against the evening sky;

all there together, heads tipped back
        to watch the Jumbotron,
all together, those whose hands laid the stones

and those who worked the looms and those
        who set fire to the brick,
the woman who stood at the sink

and the man who opened the doors,
     my son who carried the doorhangers:
all together as we heard the news, and heard

the water run again, run fast
     to the sluice gates
and beyond to the burnt wheel, turning.

Mary Leary

Venues and publications which have featured Mary's poetry and/or music include KPBS FM, KRCB FM, La Mama/La Galleria, Woodbury University, The Big Kitchen, El Campo Ruse, Creekwalker.com, ALittlePoetry.com, Arbor Vitae, Kumquat Meringue, The Melic Review, Buffalo Bones, Gypsy 3, Poetry Motel, and the wall of the girl's bathroom at Fitch Senior High; Groton, Connecticut. Her work is also in Diamonds Are a Girl's Best Friend: Women Writers on Baseball (Faber & Faber); Cher Wolfe & Other Stories (Permeable Press), Pretty Scary Jack O'Lanterns (Bread & Lightning Press), A Joyous Season (July Literary Press), The 2009 San Diego Poetry Annual (Garden Oak Press), and Hurricane Blues: Poems about Katrina and Rita (SE Missiouri State University). She writes about music for The San Diego Reader, San Diego Entertainer.com, and several other publications.

On The Bus, Early October, 2008, and What We Might Put on Our Dashboards

There is a pleasant working-class Mexican mother with children.
There is a quiet Islamic family with a daughter who nuzzles
her father's neck while eyeing
the Mexican family's precocious little girl.
There are two prostitutes, both of African descent: One
trans-gender and/or cross-dresser, one
probably born a woman. The one probably born a woman
looks prettier than the other.
We are all poor or very tired from striving not
to be poor. *Okay?* No one here
has much money.

We are all riding the bus with the loud laughing teenagers
in the back;
the thin girl who without glancing around
immediately flips her cell open;
all riding toward
the loudly lowering sun; we are
squinting or frowning
into the future.

I avoid looking west and keep
checking my watch, getting
on my own nerves. The bus
is loud, and more chaotic
than buses used to be. I am

on my way to a friend with CNN,
to watch the presidential debate in his cluttered front room
where the sleeping bag
of a man with no resources
crowds the floor.

I'd like to think everyone on the bus is going to watch the debate.
Most of us are hungry for hope.
Optimistic personalities and/or people
who were loved by their mothers and fathers
bounce along with hope like a bright rubber ball
always in their backpacks, are familiar
with it or at least don't get suicidal
from eight-plus years of indignities, fears,
environmental and political disaster.
They buy a taco and dream of God or Lego-land.

We're all poor, *okay?*
And I'd like to think we're all going to watch the debate.
Everyone to whom I've cried, "Obama 2008!" has said,
"Yes," or "Of course," has not
burst into tears of joy and relief
because he's not yet president
but if and when he is I can tell you this:

I won't have a vision of this bus driving straight
into the angry sun, a polluted Pacific,
the driver going mad at all the people piling on the bus, every day.
The often cheerful and patient bus driver won't lose it
when two more people roll their wheelchairs on,
crowding the aisles, and high-pitched phone conversations
make it hard to distinguish car horns and sirens
or just some quiet place in the driver's brain
where poor people don't just get poorer,
and sometimes

I love everyone on the bus
and I smile, like the driver. We all know
those drivers with plastic or plaster saints
on their dashboards. Now I think it's the saints
who have tiny
bus drivers on their dashboards - someone real
to whom they can pray.

Christopher Leland

Christopher Leland is a novelist, translator, literary historian, and teacher of writing. His publications include <u>Mean Time</u>, <u>The Last Happy Men: The Generation of 1922, Fiction, and the Argentine Reality</u>, <u>Open Door: Stories by Luisa Valenzuela</u> (translation), <u>The Book of Marvels</u>, and <u>Letting Loose</u>. He lives and works in Detroit, MI.

The Astonished Moment

20 January 2009

To hear you speak the words, the solemn oath,
leaves all the nations speechless, thunderstruck
at just how far we've come. To know that both
a history and world now shift forever.

Your last name seems a strange amalgam of
some Irish roots and of the Southern state
synonymous with segregation, unbeloved
for Selma, Birmingham, Montgomery scenes

of firehoses, bombs, the rifle's crack--
the signature of a whole country's shame—
today expunged by he whose lines go back
to Kenya and to Kansas—Dorothy's home—

Djakarta and Hawaii; Eagle Rock;
Columbia, to Boston; Illinois.
Whoever thought America made mock
would live to see a day like this today?

"Hussein," the Muslim caliph, and "Barak,"
the Jew and victor on Meggido's plain,
that one of Armageddon. Was it destiny or luck
that finally led you to this sacred place?

The earth has moved. The world has changed.
From everywhere, eyes turn toward you
from all those peoples—saddened, mad, estranged—
who've learned to hate us over thirty years.

From far away, across that sea of hope,
from there, the temple of our greatest man,
where Marian sang and Martin preached the scope
of our humanity, that mighty, marble statue sighed . . .
                                        and smiled.

Lyn Lifshin

Lyn Lifshin's <u>Another Woman Who Looks Like Me</u> was published by Black Sparrow at David Godine October, 2006. It has been selected for the 2007 Paterson Award for Literary Excellence for previous finalists of the Paterson Poetry Prize. Also published in 2006 was her prize winning book about the famous, short lived beautiful race horse, Ruffian:<u> The Licorice Daughter: My Year With Ruffian</u> from Texas Review Press. Lifshin's other recent books include <u>Before It's Light</u> published winter 1999-2000 by Black Sparrow press, following their publication of Cold Comfort in 1997. Just out are <u>Desire</u> from Word Parade, <u>92 Rapple Drive</u> from Coatism, <u>Persephone</u> by Red Hen, <u>Lost in the Fog</u>, and <u>Barbaro: Beyond Brokenesss </u>by Texas Review and <u>Light at the End, the Jesus Poems</u>. For other books, bio, photographs see her web site:
http://www.lynlifshin.com

On the Way to Ballroom, Private Monday Lessons

to be held. I don't need
a white close-to-strapless
dress but the arms of
someone who knows what
he's doing. Don't let
Obama's be a one night
dream of gliding and
flowing, let him hold us
close with style, let us
move not like some clod
who steps all over you,
jerks you one way then
yanks you out of yourself,
leaves a heap of what's
left of you on the floor

Sexy Is Good As Obama

he said you got to put
the two together. That
inauguration poem
didn't do it: my ball
room teacher, a man
who ought to know.
He loves Obama,
moves as he moves,
eyes on a point you
know he's going to
get to, moving smooth,
moving with grace.
I think of a cougar or
lynx slivering thru
brush and tall grass
with ease, riveting,
they seem to flow,
stealthy, muscles
rippling, taking you
along with them, sure
they are going to be
worth the way they
keep you shivering,
how your heart pounds

H. E. Mantel

H.E. Mantel/*HaroHalola*, Aquarian male, of Hallandale Beach, Florida; Poet/Writer published extensively in Print and Internet Ezines / Journals / Anthologies, including <u>Ascent Aspirations</u>, <u>Shampoo</u>, <u>Record Magazine</u>, <u>Retort</u>, <u>The Plebian Rag</u>, <u>Gloom Cupboard</u>, <u>Lit-Up Magazine</u>, <u>Writers' Bloc</u>, <u>Featuring America</u>, <u>The Apocalypse</u>, <u>A Hero's Journey Anthology</u>, <u>International War Veterans Poetry Archive</u>, <u>Poetry By Moonlight Anthology</u>, <u>Doors</u> Anthology (I & II), <u>Ambiance Artists Challenge</u> (Winner - "Betrayal"), <u>World Artist Network Magazine</u>, <u>Poetry Soup</u> (Featured Poet/Competition Award Winner, "The Pen!"), <u>Poetry Of Food Anthology</u>, <u>Poetry Of Travel Anthology</u>, <u>The National Quarterly</u>, <u>Caper</u>, <u>Eye on Life</u> (Featured Poet), <u>Animal Rights Blog</u>, <u>Talk About Cancer Anthology</u>, <u>Message In A Bottle Poetry Magazine</u>, <u>Concisely Magazine</u>; awaiting the publication of Poetry collections, *"Bananas' On The Moon...A Collection Of Revisionist Haiku"* & *"Sophistigates: A New Book Of New Poetry;"* musician-vocalist-songwriter, an avid reader, athlete, and devotee of Holistic Health through Vegan lifestyle, ecology and his Writing to Help Our Earth to Heal.

FAITHE?

What's the *Deal,* no the,
the *New*!(?) Deal? Pinned at the green
felte`, in between

B'MR's, schemers, &
Dreamers await the shuffle;
hustle-It!, they *braye*

subdueing like fit
muzzle, to the Dealer, not
unlike squealers in

demand's *Hauterote Room*
of the Amerikana
Brothotel & El

Casino Roy'lte`,
(*'cause* now, It's Black B'Jack O'
Daddie in the stage-

up), cards, like *Andrew*
'92, winding their way
in all the *ashes,*

like a *malade du*
pais de maladie du pays,
the cadastralled lull-

coze`, "Hey, ooh (*whew*) I
got 18 *showin',* deuce in
the hole..." Dealer knows,

It dealt the Cards...House

Wins so, you *lose*! No matter
Blues-Reds, the sox &

Stocks are not of your
fetes, *bleat-bleat,* only *deuce* in
the hole's *you* rolled &

Roy'lly Flushed! Break bread
with the Spade at the Diamond
Club? Be *still*, your Heart!

The Wheel-Of-Fortunes
spins in perpetuity
for The Havemores, *you*

be the primechoices,
cuts below-below..."A" deck
chairs on RMS

Titanic, touted
for grandiosity, see?
No. Of course, not. What

Wills It takes...to know
despair's selections folly-
through to muttfreedom-

wile, the loosed tether
lullcoze`afore the chainchoke;
don't be paintin' no

Crayola Rainbows
ain't *nobody* cashes chips
without camerawatch!
THEM: *The Hedgeman-
iacal Eagle ManFest,*

er, craps! Snakeyes &

slick, boxcars Willy;
you, Lowman again, again
the hard way *7-*

come-11 not,
9-11 not, the dupe's
been euchered, where're

the *Dub'yaemd's*?
"There?, There? There?" None gets
there *without* THEM! You,

'mongst the cheering
masses less-jeering PP's
(*Pacifier Part-*

ysons), thumbin' yer
ways *home...* away from the One-
Armed-Bandits stickin'

It to your slots, Jack
Potoff, go *fish*! There's some *news*
onto your Swanson's

Satellite dish, you'll
wish'd go away, what keeps
poken' yer in yer

face, hands 'n cards down!
Face-up, Jack, the Kings beat-ya
straight-out, *dubled*-down
'n dirty inta
the ground...Jack, *Zero*/Kings, *Eight,*
& counting in the

House Of Black Jack, *whack*!
& here's your *toys*, back O' the
Grand Scheme, a stringed-out

Puppet saturnale
fitrigged for *War,* & *War*, &...
'cause the more ya *see*

It, the less ya do
Nicene, Ibrihim, 'brew... an
Ecumend sec'lar

colorcoord'nate
You, not too alike? *Shrikes*! You
Bluered debaites' blur,

Butcherbirds own your
loggerheads, *fiskaals* for the
hangman's game?, you'll get

Grey-not-Great! It's not
about the *how* of handshakes,
rather the *why, Guiy*!

But their black & red
ruselette, funspun on the odd
chances, & the yous

Keeblings, *liebling* a
budget f'that ultra-fudgy
Mandala jam pie
High-antied-up in
rarified heir, break *naan* with
the Spade at the Black

Diamond Club. Be *still,*
your Heart!, be still for the diss-
illusion; for *the*

need always larger
than the man, the antivote
an anodyne...& yous

Prime! "Ya want fries with
that?" The parvmenu, hyp-hop-
crisy, now; the raced

for The Fragrancy?
Nary a *Race,* 'cept...this co-
verture groom, doffed

'n coiffed, suited/un-
suited, the *suavte*`same, blank
stares & blank checks &

balances... Stern &
Bearer grins, junkets to *craps*!,
as little Joe fades...

But THEM not of a
colorblindness, oh no, *No*!
Furtive *REM*

Like *non plus ultras,*
furledchurlchuff attenutive
to the scuff & scruff...
thy evergreening
Amerika (*do* Xmas!),
in Thanksgoing, *yea,*

frankly, & some deep-

ditch apple pie, whilst... "Hey, now
we cain't put 'em (*all*)

inta the *Ghrabe*, who's
gonna dig, Niccolo?" So...
BOMO! You had a

dream, & that's *It!* A
little freedom's something *left*
to lose... Cerber-us,

in rev'lry's ensue
if *change* goes down we'll feel the
byte, might not lose the

full house? So, *BOMO*
stringed-out Plotitics for the
strunghungout, a *merci-*

beau-coup in
absconders wake to truss the
rupture, Finnegan,

after the rape, like
kitteners what never pause a
mirror to stop &

reflect... It's in the
bag! Swine's imargination.
See? No. Of course, not?
Dis pair, *Partis Pro
Mitigo lentus Neo-
Pubs,* the Doverdel

of Celtichuff &
his smile of Capri, yea the

gaggle of the *Four*

R's, in service to
the *renegade's* secret, that
radiancerosebud

ain't a toboggan
for calefaction; Texas
(*Whuse-saene*?)

Hold-'em & fold-'em
based-on-balls? Yo' Daddie yo'
Mama! *The GAME* grinds-on, *wronged*

Players/*Ownerules*
& *you* on the Spit!, dressed like
a *logot - BOMO*

#44 - & kids
named B'racky, *all* tryin' for
Lefty...& unarmed

bandits, so slick...makes
pale Dick's tricks, don'cha know, Joe?
'Bout *profligate, &*

the crapulous? Hey,
It's a "*New* American
Century," a *rude*
Enciteclopaedic
paged by a *Gangle Of Four*!
For the defend of

the Enemies both
Domestic &, *Domestic*...
The sad & sodden,

Trumped! Junior Duo-
poly's the *man*, all right, *Srouji!*
Yeah, we got *PO'd*

The *New*!(?) Deal? Pinned at
the green *felte`*, in between
B'MR's, schemers, &

Dreamers...on 'nother
iced, toll bridge to nowhere, chats
for chits' *BetterScheme*

as the *Jokers* run
a mukluk, Vice-begets-Vice
but you ain't *prezy*,

You what have, w*rackers,*
not the vegast *tell* why the
Machines this time *fixed*?

> *H.e.m.*/H'H
> 11.8.MMviii.
> (*ST*)

Helene McGlauflin

Helene McGlauflin, MEd, LCPC, KYT is a counselor, educator, writer and yoga teacher. Helene currently is a school counselor at a public elementary school, teaches yoga to children and adults, and writes fiction, nonfiction and poetry when she can. Her work has appeared in small presses, professional journals, magazines, books and newspapers. Helene has two adult children and lives with her husband Bruce in Bath, Maine.

African American History
Month Exhibit
Philadelphia Constitution Center,
January 2009

This diminutive dark skinned woman holds
a crumpled white tissue in her wrinkled hand
that rhythmically moves from eyes to nose,
mouth to sleeve, then habitually tucked, ready.
Owl glasses frame her face, press close to display
cases ensuring every word is read, every image
seen, all tears honored

I am an accidental witness behind her, drowning
under a tidal wave of sorrow as we crawl past
fuzzy pictures, neck chains, whips, dark chambers,
my skin white as the KKK hood, my shame so deep.
Are my tears worthy? Standing finally by her side
surrounded by throaty songs of defiance and faith
we shed tears of no color, we, the crumpled tissue
soaked, shredded and saved by all that was, is

Corey Mesler

COREY MESLER is the owner of Burke's Book Store in Memphis, Tennessee. He has published poetry and prose in hundreds of journals. He has two novels published by Livingston Press, <u>Talk: a Novel in Dialogue</u>, and <u>We are Billion-Year-Old Carbon</u>. He also has a full length poetry collection, <u>Some Identity Problems</u>, and a book of short stories, <u>Listen</u>, available, plus over a dozen chapbooks. He has two more novels due out in March of 2010. He has had two poems on Garrison Keillor's <u>Writer's Almanac</u>. Most importantly he is Cheryl's husband, and Toby and Chloe's dad. He can be found at http://www.coreymesler.com.

Obama

Now is the time for hope.
We must say so.
We have dined on gargoyles
and crow. We have
seen the sky turn orange,
the sea black. We
have lived enough in ignorance
calling it homeland.
We have bathed in oil because
they told us it was milk.
Now is the time for hope.
We welcome again the open book,
the open hand.
And we say *we* again, the many,
the unfurling crowd,
the long line back to the sun.

Luci Mistratov

Luci Mistratov was born in Kaliningrad, Russia and holds a Ph.D. in art education. She has illustrated many books of fiction and science, taught art and won awards in numerous national and international exhibitions in Europe and the United States. http://www.mycolorworld.net

Birthday

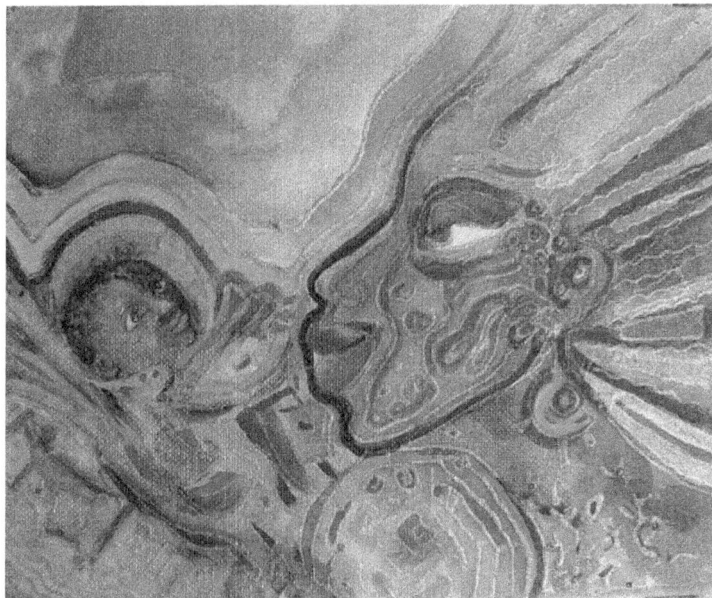

Eric G. Müller

Eric G. Müller was born in Durban, South Africa, and studied literature and history at the University of Witwatersrand, Johannesburg. After a few years working at a variety of jobs, playing and performing music, and traveling around Europe, he attended Emerson College in Sussex, England and the Waldorf Institute in Witten-Annen, Germany, where he specialized in music education. Together with his family he moved to Eugene, Oregon, where he taught for eight years. Currently he is living in upstate New York, teaching music, drama, English literature and creative writing. He is a founding member of the Alkion Center and is the director of the education department. He has taught at Simon's Rock College of Bard as an adjunct teacher and summer courses at Sunbridge College. His novel Rites of Rock (Adonis 2005) is a fast-moving and riveting saga that examines the phenomenon of rock music. In Coffee on the Piano for You Müller presents old and new poetry written mostly while traveling or drinking coffee. His second novel, Meet Me at the Met will appear in the early spring of 2010 (Plain View Press). His website is: http://www.ericgmuller.com

Election (Honoring the historic election of 11/04/08)

At the eleventh hour,
Seconds after the lapidary announcement
By the late night anchor man was made,
I was shoved down onto the piano stool
And told to play, while the crowd whooped
And chanted, "Play, play, play!"

My mind went stone blank and
The moment stretched into a mile
While my fingers stroked the ivory coast,
Overpowered by the music I was supposed to make
To underscore the monumental event,
Pushed by a crowd high with hope.

My fingers took over and sailed across the black
And white keys, with a slow, slow blues that launched
A hundred thousand slavers into the salt-soaked desert,
While my right hand witnessed their tortured passage across,
And my left hand's relentless beat saw them sold and separated,
In a rampage of wails and cries, calls and hollers, shouts and shrieks.

I played on through the centuries, paying homage
To all the hurt ever uttered by the abused minority
Under the pale yoke of savage discrimination –
Till quite warmed up I broke the chains of bondage
To the chant of, "Yes we can," – and shifted to a major key,

As the man, Barack Obama, truly chosen by sure majority
Stepped up to accept a hard earned triumph for humanity!

Bennett Paris

Bennett Paris lives in Salvador, Bahia, Brazil, where he makes a semblance of a living as a translator, tour guide, and English teacher.

Obama T-Shirt in Brazil

They waited in line while the fried bean cakes called *acarajé* sizzled in a vat of red-brown palm oil. A stranger leaned between them and said, "It looks so good."

"Smells good too." Myrna said. It was the first English outside the airport they'd heard since they arrived in Salvador da Bahia. Black Rome the city was called, according to the guidebook, because of the African influence and the hundreds of Catholic churches.

"She's the best, apparently," Myrna continued, pointing to the woman in the white lace headdress and matching gown, flipping the *acarajé* that floated in the oil.

Myrna and her husband, Dr. Emmanuel Rose, turned around to see who she was speaking to.

"That's what I've heard also." Round horn-rimmed glasses, head shaved, he looked like Gandhi but taller and heavier.

"This is my second time," the woman standing next to him said. She leaned into her husband; he put his arm around her in response. All four of them laughed together, not because anything was particularly funny, but because they were becoming friends.

"I'll take a schmear of that," Dr. Rose said. It was their turn on line. The *acarajé* vendor filled the steaming bean cakes with a pumpkin-colored stuffing they found out later was called vatapá.

"A schmear. Ha! It's just like Zabar's," the husband said.

They all laughed again. Dr. Rose was pleased that his new American friend understood his reference.

Between the "ooohs" and the "aaahs" at the *acarajé,* their introductions, and the discovery that they were all from the suburbs of New York, they agreed, the two couples, Dr. Emmanuel Rose and Myrna, Scott and Adelle, to take a table together across the street. Cradling their food with both hands, they navigated the traffic, and found an empty table under the giant mango tree in the square.

Scott gestured at the waiter for a beer, his two index fingers, one on top of the other, indicating the approximate height of a beer bottle. "That's pretty good," Dr. Rose said. "You're learning the local lingo."

"Even if it is sign language," Scott completed the thought.

"Hey look," Myrna said. She pointed across the street. "That's the first time I've seen that down here." A man was wearing an Obama 2008 t-shirt. It was July, a few months before the election.

"We're very excited about it," Myrna said.

"Everyone is," Scott said. "Look." He pointed at the man in the Obama t-shirt again. "Even Brazilians."

Myrna waved at the man in the Obama shirt, trying to get his attention.

"He's concentrating on his *acarajé,*" Dr. Rose said. "He won't notice you."

"As long as he votes," Scott said, "it doesn't matter." They laughed again.

A vendor selling hammocks approached the table. "I've always wanted a hammock," she said. The vendor stopped.

"Me too," Scott's wife, Adelle, said. She pointed at an orange hammock in the pile slung over the vendor's shoulder.

The vendor recited a price, and added something else.

"What did he say?"

"Seventy *reais*," Scott said.

"I understood that part," Myrna said. "High school Spanish. Numbers are pretty much the same in Portuguese. But after that?"

They looked at each other and shrugged.

"He said the hammocks are hand-made and will last a half of a lifetime," a voice from the next table said.

"Oh," Myrna said. "Half a lifetime? I guess it depends how long you live." The group chortled.

They looked at the translator. Legs crossed, self-effacing smile, stringy brown hair hanging over his forehead, oval wire-rimmed glasses, his head was shaped like a hatchet.

The vendor said something else.

"He said they have more over there." The translator pointed at a woman across the street. She rested her arm on a chair piled high with colorful hammocks.

"Oh wow. Can we go over and look?" Myrna said.

"Sure," the translator said. He barked something at the vendor.

Myrna and Adelle stood up and walked toward the hammocks. The vendor followed. When they were gone, the translator held out his hand.

"Dente," he said. He pronounced it "DEN-chee."

"Manny," Dr. Rose said. "And this is Scott." They shook.

"Funny name." Scott said.

"Nickname. It means 'tooth.'" Dente smiled. "See." He showed them his large pointy canines. "My real name is Roland, but I'm the only one around here who knows that. I resisted in the beginning, tried to explain that I prefer Roland to Dente, got angry even when people insisted. But they love cruel nicknames here. If you have big ears, they'll call you "Ears." I know someone called "Crab" because he was born with a deformed hand that looked like a crab claw."

"Roland is fine with us." Dr. Rose looked over at Scott.

"Sure. Roland is ok."

"I'm used to Dente. I don't care anymore. I don't want to be tempted anyway."

"Tempted?" Dr. Rose said.

"Tempted to deceive myself into expecting the dignity that deserves a real name."

"Come on," Scott said. "It can't be that bad."

"You couldn't know. Twenty-five years here. Let's change the subject," Dente said. Then he added, "So you're just passing through?"

"A few days," Dr. Rose said.

"Same here," Scott said. "We're just tourists."

"I know. Your socks," Dente said to Dr. Rose. "No one here wears socks."

Dr. Rose scanned the ankles around him.

"I wonder where he got that shirt," Scott said. He pointed to the man wearing the Obama shirt.

"His son lives in California. I know the guy," Dente said. "And you're from?"

"We're Americans," Dr. Rose said.

"North Americans, you mean."

"Technically, yes," Scott said. "Sure."

"Brazilians think of themselves as Americans too, but South Americans."

"So then, I guess we're all Americans, North and South," Dr. Rose said. "You're German, I'd say by your accent."

"Close," Dente said. He lit a cigarette.

"Swiss," Scott said. "I met a Swiss guy up at the fisherman's colony the other day."

"Kurt." Dente said. "I know him. Came for a visit, married one of the fisherman's daughters, and never went back."

"Which means you're from...?" Scott said.

"I'm a citizen of the world," Dente said. "I have no passport."

"No passport?" Scott and Dr. Rose exchanged glances.

"Long story. Another night," Dente said.

"But if you had a passport...?"

"Guess," Dente said.

"Hungary. Croatia. I have no idea," Scott said.

Dente looked at Dr. Rose, who shrugged.

"Deep in the heart of Europe."

"Suit yourself," Dr. Rose said.

"Do you realize," Dente said, "that until World War I passports didn't exist?" He nodded with a friendly enthusiasm. "You could go wherever in the world you wanted. That's right. No passports, no visas. Imagine a world like that?"

"Hardly." Scott poured beer into Dr. Rose's glass, then his own, until there was none left in the bottle. The waiter placed another bottle of beer on the table.

"I'll have a Cuba Livre," Dente said to the waiter, looking from Dr. Rose to Scott and back to Dr. Rose, "you don't mind, do you?"

"Not at all. It'll be my pleasure," Scott said.

"Sure," Dr. Rose said, "our pleasure." Then, "I wasn't aware of that either, no passports before the First World War."

"You wouldn't," Dente said, and smiled. "Typically American."

"North American, you mean."

"No. American. Brazilians are just as oblivious."

"Oblivious?'' Dr. Rose looked over at Scott for support.

"There's no history here. You're all oblivious; oblivious to history, oblivious to reality. Bush. Iraq. Where do you think that comes from? Total oblivion."

"No arguments from me about that," Dr. Rose said. "I'm ashamed of it, the disaster in Iraq. I hate to say this, but it makes me ashamed to be American sometimes."

"Me too," Scott said. "What a mess over there."

Dente continued. "Brazilians, Americans. All the same."

"That's an exaggeration," Dr. Rose said.

"Innocent, optimistic; everything's always great, isn't it?" Dente continued.

Dr. Rose and Scott looked at each other.

"Things aren't bad, now that you mention it," Dr. Rose finally said. "Could always use a little more money, but other than that..." He noticed Myrna and her new friend, Adelle, across the street. They had drifted from the hammocks to a store-front window display of clothing from India. One of the things Dr. Rose admired about Myrna was how easily she made new friends.

"As long as you're not Black," Dente broke up laughing as if he'd just delivered a coup de grâce. The waiter brought his drink, rum in a glass filled with ice, and a can of Coca-Cola. Dente snapped open the can and poured Coke into the glass.

"The Europeans, of course, know nothing about racism, right? A perfect society you have over there," Dr. Rose said.

"That's right. Everything Americans are trying to be."

"As long as you're not Jewish," Dr. Rose said, retaliating. It was against his better judgment, and he regretted it instantly.

"The Jews. Ha! Always talking about the Jews. Look at the world today. If it weren't for the Jews there'd be no war in the world. Iraq, and soon Iran, all of it because of Israel. They have no business in Palestine. You're probably a Zionist, aren't you? Zionism, racism, it's all the same."

Dr. Rose seethed.

Dente sipped his drink, smiling.

Scott said, "Wait a second. Wait a second. That's not a fair thing to say."

"What do you know?" Dente said. "You'll do or say anything to fit in. I've met plenty of Black Americans passing through here; typical Uncle Tom, seems like to me. Oreo, as they say." Dente laughed again, doubling over in feigned glee.

"Enough," Dr. Rose said.

Dente looked at his drink. "See. Can't stand to hear the truth, can you? Classic American."

"Truth?" Dr. Rose leaned toward Dente. "Bullshit you mean. Go on. Get out of here. Take your drink and leave." He spoke calmly, but he found himself trembling with rage. Dr. Rose had been in a physical fight once in his adult life. An undergraduate at a frat-house nightclub, Dr. Rose remembers grappling his adversary to the ground, and grabbing him by the adam's apple with his left hand, pressed his neck into the sidewalk, and pummeled him with his right, smashing blows on the temple, nose, and cheek. Dr. Rose let up only when he realized the guy was no longer defending himself. He felt the same rage for Dente as he did that night and he was afraid about what he might do.

Dente opened his mouth to speak.

"One more word and I'll tear your throat out of your neck. You understand?" Dr. Rose spoke deliberately, without raising his voice. He put his hands on the table, preparing to stand up. "One more word."

Dente crossed his legs. He had a smug smile on his face that made Dr. Rose angrier. Myrna and Adelle returned.

"Beautiful stuff," Myrna said. Everyone at the table was silent.

"I'm not allowed to talk," Dente said.

"Manny?" Myrna addressed him with the tone of voice she reserved for serious situations.

"Go on," Dr. Rose said to Dente. "Leave." He pushed his chair back. "Don't make me stand up."

"Manny?"

"Get out of here." Scott said to Dente. "Now."

Dente poured the rest of the Coke can into his glass. "Typical," Dente said, walking away. "Oblivious," he said, baring his teeth.

After he was gone, Myrna said, "What was that all about, honey?"

Dr. Rose and Scott both had their arms crossed. They were shaking their heads back and forth. "Do you believe that guy?" Dr. Rose said. "We're trying to enjoy our vacation, a nice night out, new friends..."

"Unbelievable," Scott said. "Absolutely unbelievable."

"I probably shouldn't have threatened him," Dr. Rose said to Scott. Then to Myrna, "I just threatened that guy."

"He crossed the line," Scott said.

"He did, didn't he? But we were just talking, really." Dr. Rose was still trembling.

"Talk to me, honey." Myrna stood in front of him. Her eyes were blinking fast.

"But where does he come off saying that kind of stuff?" Dr. Rose said.

"Hateful bitter platitudes. We've seen it before," Scott said. "As if he gets off on it, somehow."

Adelle sat down next to him. Myrna sat next to her.

"Not sure what started it, but before we knew it that guy was blasting everything we know," Scott said. "Just taking us apart."

"It makes you realize..." Dr. Rose said to three other Americans at the table. "It makes you realize, doesn't it?" He lost his train of thought when he noticed Dente a few tables away hovering near a couple wearing socks.

"Realize what?" Myrna said.

"This visceral response...," Dr. Rose said.

"...To that kind of nonsense," Scott looked at his wife and Myrna, then at Dr. Rose. "Pure hateful garbage," Scott said. "But maybe there's something about us now...Americans."

"Something about us," Dr. Rose said, "that won't let us put up with it anymore." Dr. Rose glanced from face to face. "We just won't fucking put up with it anymore, that kind of intolerance, will we?" It felt good to swear; he articulated the word "fucking" with an awkward precision. "And we're all the same that way. We, Americans. We have to come to the other side of the world to realize it. But it's true."

"It's something good about us," Scott said. "Iraq, Bush, true, an embarrassment. But this, maybe this is something to be proud of...this visceral response, as you put it, to that kind of garbage."

"But he said you didn't let him talk," Myrna said.

"He talked plenty," Scott said.

"Plenty," Dr. Rose said.

Louis Phillips

Louis Phillips, a widely published poet, playwright, and short story writer, has written some 35 books for children and adults. Among his works are: three collections of short stories—<u>A Dream of Countries Where No One Dare To Live</u> (SMU Press), <u>The Bus to the Moon</u> (Fort Schuyler Press), and <u>The Woman Who Wrote King Lear and Other Stories</u> (Pleasure Boat Studio). His collection of stories, poems, humor pieces and a full-length play – <u>The Fireworks in Some Particulars</u> -- will be published in the Spring of 2010 by Forth Schuyler Press.

The Night Obama Was Elected President of the United States

The night Obama was elected President
My wife & I walked toward Columbia University
To greet students spilling out into the street,
Singing, hand clapping, an entire city
Wide awake with life-affirming carryings-on.
Coleridge's "Passion of Hope" made evident.
For once, the tide of History was with us,
Rapidly rising, running in, then out, as
We went sailing down Broadway at dawn.

T. R. Poulson

T. R. Poulson grew up on a farm near American Falls, Idaho. She now lives in Reno, works at UPS, and studies at the University of Nevada. When she's not reading or writing, she enjoys windsurfing, kickboxing, horseback riding, running, and playing basketball.

She Wants to Be President

She says (while smiling, winking with her words)
"We're mavericks." Unbranded orphan calves. No?
"We'll lower taxes." And a line I've never heard

from any politician in the past: "Look forward,
darn it, not back. Say it ain't so, Joe,"
she says, while smiling. Winking, after her words.

And just who's causing our warming world?
The orphan calves? She doesn't seem to *know*.
"We'll lower taxes," Again. I've never heard

that victory in Iraq is within sight. A blurred
memory: *Mission Accomplished*. "Oh, no,"
she thinks. While smiling, winking, without words,

she glances at her cards, for the unheard
coaching of her running mate. *There we go*:
"Lower taxes." One thing I've often heard

is orphan calves are cute, away from the herd.
Cowboys feed them bottled milk, their eyes glow.
She says, while smiling and winking at her words:
"We'll lower taxes." A line I've *never* heard.

Marian Shapiro

Marian Kaplun Shapiro is the author of a professional book, <u>Second Childhood</u> (Norton, 1988), a poetry book, <u>Players In The Dream</u>, <u>Dreamers In The Play</u> (Plain View Press, 2007) and two chapbooks: <u>Your Third Wish</u>, (Finishing Line, 2007); and <u>The End Of The World, Announced On Wednesday</u> (Pudding House, 2007). As a Quaker and a psychologist, her poetry often addresses the embedded topics of peace and violence, often by addressing one within the context of the other. Born and raised in The Bronx, she has been a resident of Lexington, MA since the age of 25. She also won the Senior Poets Laureate Poetry Competition for the state of Massachusetts in 2006 and again in 2008.

An Occasional Poem*
for Barack Obama,
on Inauguration Day, 2009

In the moment when
everything comes together, when
the picture emerges, when
the artist knows it's done, when
all that remains is to sign the canvas:
Real, it sings, *this is real.*
Nothing will ever be the same again.

---

* A poem written for a particular occasion, such as a
dedication, birthday, or victory

Noel Sloboda

Noel Sloboda lives in Pennsylvania, where he teaches at Penn State York and serves as dramaturg for the Harrisburg Shakespeare Festival.

"Summer Before the Election" has been published previously by sunnyoutside in <u>Stages</u>, and it is included here with permission from the publisher.

Summer before the Election

All the Shakespeare festivals ran
Julius Caesar and *Richard II* nonstop.
Yet we wanted Arden—and women

who acted like men (who reminded us
they were once played by boys
who performed before a woman

who had more power than any man).
Instead, we got countless curses,
bad dreams, men who acted liked boys,

slashes delivered by high-minded assassins.
At the end of the season, tired
of togas, Pomfret, and rhetoric,

we'd have settled for almost anything
lighter, even that play with the bear,
so long as he danced the drobushki.

Paul Sohar

Paul Sohar got to pursue his life-long interest in literature full time when he went on disability from his job in a chemistry lab. The results have slowly showed up in <u>Chiron</u>, <u>Grain</u>, <u>Homestead Review</u>, <u>International Poetry Review</u>, <u>Kenyon Review</u>, <u>Main Street Rag</u>, <u>Poem</u>, <u>Poesy</u>, <u>Poetry Motel</u>, <u>Rattle</u>, <u>Slant</u>, <u>Wordwrights</u>, etc., and seven books of translations from the Hungarian. Now a volume of his own poetry (<u>Homing Poems</u>) is available from Iniquity Press. His latest work is <u>True Tales of a Fictitious Spy</u>, a creative nonfiction book about the Stalinist gulag in Hungary. He is a frequent speaker at MLA and other conferences.

To a Candidate Offering Tomorrow on Sale

you're farting through your ears
and eyes
not only through your mouth

you're making the air around you sick
the posters on the wall are falling down faint
throwing up
and letting go a rambling train of sewage

a smell i'd never get to know without your
sticky-handed solicitude
i don't want to be rude but i've got to hold
my stomach and can't shake your hand

even your pockets and socks are overflowing
your collar is choking itself in disgust
and if you call this a dream you're welcome to it
for me the election's over

let me out i'll pay the price
as long as i don't have to hold
or handle whatever it is you're selling

Margaret Vidale

Margaret Vidale has lived in the suburbs of Boston for over 40 years. She began writing poetry after retiring from teaching in 2001. Many of her early poems were description and expressions of the severe abuse she survived as a child. She found writing about the violence in her family to be healing and empowering. Now, in her senior years, those crushing childhood memories are balanced by the joy of watching her grandsons grow and thrive in a loving home. Margaret's poems have appeared in <u>Pearl</u>, <u>South Boston Literary Gazette</u>, <u>Tapestries</u>, <u>Lucid Rhythms</u>, <u>Avocet</u> and other small press publications.

This piece was inspired by the quote "Rosa sat so Martin could walk so Barack could run". This was a quote widely used in 2008 in a wide range of contexts without attribution of the name of the source. An attempt has been made to dig more into the actual original source of this quote, and some additional discussion on that follows after the piece.

All Over the Globe

 Walking along the Charles River,
my feet catch the rhythm of children chanting¬¬¬—
"Rosa sat so Martin could walk so Barack could run!"*
With each step, a name¬¬—Rosa, Martin, Barack,

Rosa Parks, if could ride that Montgomery bus,
I'd bend my arthritic back
onto the seat next to you,
link my long, white arm
through your small, dark one
and pull your quilt of determination
around us both.
Sisters, I'd whisper.

Many oppress us—
bully bus drivers, alcoholic fathers,
white supremacists parading Nazi uniforms.
You protest with a personal sit-in,
I use my poet's pen
to document abuses long buried.

I'm the grandmother of two blended boys;
they skype-dance in their Lexington living room
for Mah Mah and Yeh Yeh in Hong Kong.
You are the mother of the Civil Rights Movement;
your grandchildren sing and dance all over the globe—
on Boston streets, in Paris cafes and Prague
bookstores;

they skip across Jakarta school grounds
and Kogelo courtyards.

I honor your choice, Rosa,
to stay and suffer the consequences.
You refused to move,
so our rainbow descendents
might walk, run, leap and soar.

* This piece was inspired by the quote "Rosa sat so Martin could walk so Barack
could run". The origin of this quote is not clear.
This NPR story: http://www.npr.org/templates/story/story.php?storyId=96215190
indicates the quote originated from an unnamed source who sent a text message
to an instructor of "Manufacturing Training Alliance".

This source: http://www.dailykos.com/story/2008/10/29/15143/556/908/645922
raises the possibility that the quote originated from Jay-Z in an October 2008
concert.

Johanna Wald

Johanna Wald is a freelance writer. Her essays and articles have appeared in <u>The Externalist</u>, <u>MotherVerse</u>, <u>Pilgrimage Magazine</u>, <u>The Boston Globe</u>, <u>Education Week</u> and <u>The Nation</u>. Her memoir, entitled "One Brief Shining Moment" was awarded by the editors of Pilgrimage as the best essay of 2008 published in that magazine. She has also written guest blogs for the political column "Stark Ravings" of the <u>Boston Phoenix</u>.

Exorcising the Ghosts of Elections Past

From Labor Day until November 4, I felt like I was holding my breath. The mostly positive polls, at least from early October on, actually heightened my anxiety. Even as I began to smell victory, I fretted over the fallout from yet another disappointment. My mood fluctuated wildly minute by minute between fear and hope, doubt and faith, often as a result of miniscule shifts in the daily tracking polls, which I followed obsessively. I had dueling mantras running through my head at all times. "Yes we can" was competing for psychic space with my now habitual sense of foreboding: "this will end badly."

I was not alone. I heard many express similar sentiments, especially those of us who seem to carry the trauma of past electoral defeats in our genes. We suffer from a chronic condition which I have dubbed "Post Election Stress Syndrome," or PESS. If you are a lifelong Democrat like me, PESS, with three exceptions, has resurfaced every four years for the past 40 years. Each person, of course, experiences this phenomenon in his or her own idiosyncratic way, but common symptoms include depression, despair, anger, and resignation; often accompanied by sudden bouts of tears. We often quietly curse the demographic group of the hour—the soccer or security moms, NASCAR dads, "Reagan Democrats," right-wing evangelicals— credited with providing the margin of victory to our opponents. We have created a permanent villain hall of fame consisting of Katherine Harris, Kenneth Blackwell, Karl Rove, hanging chads, butterfly ballots and Diebold machines. A few weeks after an election, you might find us talking secession of the coastal states around the water cooler, or noting the similarities between the pre-Civil War slave/free state map and the red/blue divide of the electoral college. When the acute anger passes, many of us remain bereft that our vision for the country seems to be at odds with so much of the country.

The original source of this trauma, for me, can be traced back to 1968, when I was 12 years old. I lived in a suburb of Washington D.C. My father worked on Robert Kennedy's Presidential campaign. All spring, I had campaigned ferociously for my candidate amongst my friends, many of whom supported Humphrey or McCarthy. After Martin Luther King was assassinated, I felt like only Bobby could bring the country back together. My father returned from California the night before that state's primary. I drifted to sleep praying to God for a Kennedy victory, and was jolted awake at 5:00 a.m. by a phone call from my grandmother telling us that he had been assassinated. To this day, if the phone rings early in the morning, I flash back to that moment. The summer after RFK was killed, I remember a gloom descending upon my family like the oppressive humidity that blankets Washington in the summer. I have never been able to approach a campaign since without a sense of dread; the more I care about a candidate, the more I brace myself for the inevitable heartbreak to come.

Needless to say, I have woken up feeling miserable on far more Wednesdays in November than I care to recall. The most devastating in recent memory came on November 3, 2004, when my bleary-eyed nine year old daughter appeared at the top of the stairs at about 7:00 a.m. and asked me: "Mommy, who won the election?" Only hours before, I had bid good night to her in a cheery and optimistic mood, buoyed by exit polls indicating a Kerry win. After a very long night, however, Kerry's anticipated votes in Ohio did not materialize, nor did the much ballyhooed "youth vote." Trying to keep myself from curling up into a fetal position on the floor as I contemplated the next four years under Bush/Cheney, I looked up at her and responded in as matter of fact a tone as possible; "I think George W. Bush won." My daughter rushed downstairs and hugged me: "Mommy, I am so sorry." With her words, all of the frustration, anger and sensation of being sucker punched that had been building all night came gushing out of me. I burst into tears and cried on and off for the next week. Later that morning, I walked grimly in a cold and dreary rain around the Brookline Reservoir, unable to make eye contact with any of the other dispirited souls circling the path, thinking about the misery certain to be inflicted on all of us for the next four years.

PESS has become so deeply embedded into my DNA that I have lost the capacity to make a clear-eyed assessment of my candidates' prospects. I am simply too spooked by the ghosts of losses past. In 2006, I did not trust any of the polls that pointed toward large Democratic gains in the House and Senate. Until the networks announced the outcome, I was convinced that the Republicans would somehow swoop down and steal those votes away to create the permanent majority of Karl Rove's dreams.

Despite my best efforts to stay emotionally aloof during the 2008 Presidential primaries, I found myself pulled in by the energy, vision, and stirring rhetoric of Barack Obama. The more I watched, the more I really liked this guy. I liked what he said, the way that he said it, and the manner in which he conducted himself. I loved listening to the cadences of his voice when he spoke. He would begin in a calm, measured tone as if to quiet the crowd, and then build to his climax, when the audience would jump to its feet. I gave up whatever resistance lingered within me when he made his speech on race relations in April. As I listened to his deep, nuanced analysis, I could not believe that a person of this intelligence and thoughtfulness might actually become our President. What, I imagined, would it be like to listen to him for the next four years?

My growing attachment to Obama scared the hell out of me. Adding to my anxieties were these eerie similarities between the campaigns of 1968 and 2008. In both years, an unpopular war divided the Democratic Party, sparking a bruising Presidential primary campaign. As the spring wore on, the increasingly vitriolic tenor of the race threatened to spill over into the convention, throwing the Party into disarray and hobbling its prospects for victory in the fall. Many whispered in hushed tones their fears about violence and assassination.

But then this funny thing happened. Events that veered so tragically wrong in 1968 went astonishingly right in 2008. The primaries ended peacefully. When Obama emerged the victor, his chief rival, Hillary Clinton, endorsed and campaigned for him. The Democratic National Convention, the scene of bloodshed and violence in 1968, offered in 2008 an almost flawless display of party unity. After Obama's magnificent speech in Denver, I yielded to a moment of optimism. Maybe, this time, the best candidate would actually win.

As usual, my hopefulness was short-lived. It lasted less than a day. The next morning, McCain selected Sarah Palin as his running mate. Very quickly, the confidence I had felt gave way to fear and panic. I was in good company. Anyone who paid even marginal attention to last fall's campaign could literally feel the palpable hysteria running rampant among Obama supporters right after the Republican convention. In those first weeks of September, Palin appeared to be an inspired choice. McCain's campaign staff attacked Obama with gleeful abandon, Biden seemed to be knocked off his stride, and Obama's decision not to put Hillary on the ticket looked like a fatal miscalculation. I remember waking up to a *USA Today* poll showing McCain leading Obama 54 percent to 44 percent, and feeling the blood rush from my face. "Oh my God," I thought, "this is Dukakis/Bush all over again." McCain started to pick up steam in key states: he lead North Carolina, once considered competitive, by 20 points, was going toe to toe with Obama in Michigan, where Obama had recently enjoyed a 10 point advantage, and started to pull ahead in New Hampshire. Many of us felt that the Obama campaign had become too slow and halting in its responses.

Before our horrified eyes, we started to imagine Obama morph into Hubert Humphrey, George McGovern, Walter Mondale, Michael Dukakis, Al Gore and John Kerry, all bundled up into one LOSER package.

During those dark days, I surprised myself by discovering steel in my spine. Instead of going limp with resignation, I rose up to repeat Obama's cry during his convention speech: "Not this time." I, along with my fellow weary, frightened, fatalistic and determined warriors, sprang into action, working phone banks, canvassing door to door, registering votes, sending in donations we could not afford, and demanding that the media call out McCain for his lies and distortions. That was the visible stuff. In the privacy of our homes, offices, bedrooms and cars, we also indulged in any activity or ritual—no matter how ridiculous, silly or nonsensical—that we believed would keep positive karmic energy flowing in Obama's direction. Even before the economic meltdown, McCain's fateful utterance that the "fundamentals of our economy are strong," Palin's incoherent mutterings to Charlie Gibb and Katie Couric, and Obama's emergence in the face of economic tumult as a reasoned, disciplined, and reassuring leader, the polls had started shifting back to our guy. I know because I was tracking them, second by second. I am convinced that the tremendous amount of psychic will and energy generated by "we the Democrats who have been burned too often before" played some role in bringing about that shift.

Throughout the rest of the campaign, I barely made a move without thinking through its electoral implications. I became inordinately superstitious, particularly about the relationship between sports and politics. I was acutely aware that the Red Sox had won the World Series in 2004, just a week before Kerry lost the election. Therefore, I figured that they had to be sacrificed this year to a higher cause—an Obama victory. When they fended off elimination during the fifth game of the championship series against Tampa Bay, rallying to overcome a 7-0 deficit, I fretted instead of rejoicing. What if their "rise from the dead" comeback foreshadowed a late-inning McCain resurgence? Secretly, because I live in a household of Sox fans, I sighed in relief when they lost the series two games later. Similarly, I willed defeat upon my beloved childhood football team, the Washington Redskins, on the eve of the election. History shows that a Redskins loss right before the election bodes well for the challenging party. Even if my brothers and father would never forgive me, I felt reluctantly compelled to wish a resounding loss upon them that night.

By that last, frantic week, I was leaving nothing to chance. Because I had taken election day off in 2004, I went into work on November 4, 2008. I refused to cut my hair until after the election. I had plenty of company in my tortured logic. When I decided, with about a week to go, that I needed to be more positive, my mother, perhaps even more fatalistic than me, chided: "Don't you dare! Your negativity has worked very well so far, don't screw things up by going positive now." My oldest friend, who shared a few Democratic defeats with me in our childhood, later admitted she had deliberately stayed away from me all fall, fearing that our collective anxiety might tilt the karmic balance toward McCain. She also refused to wear any clothes that she had owned in 2004. On election night, she wouldn't even sit on the couch upon which she had watched the 2004 returns.

Another friend decided to schedule her dog to be spayed on election day. "Is that a good idea?" I asked. "Oh yes," she assured me, "Don't you get it? The dog represents McCain, who will also be neutered that day." I wasn't sure if I totally followed that reasoning, but I trusted that she had thought through the implications on Obama's prospects.

In the days leading to the election, in my world, talk turned distinctly mystical. One colleague spoke of an impending tsunami—in a good sense. Once the wave—that being an Obama victory—actually broke, he sensed a flooding of relief and euphoria would wash over all of us. On the evening before the election, my cousin distressed me when she mentioned the prediction of an astrologist friend of an "upset" on November 4. After much discussion, however, we determined that an "upset" to an astrologist means a planetary realignment, not a reversal of a few Rasmussen or Gallup poll numbers. And that had to mean only one thing: an Obama victory. At least that's how we convinced ourselves to interpret her prediction.

None of this, however, really reassured me. I was an emotional wreck all election day, paying particular attention to reported voting problems in Virginia. When early returns from that state tilted toward McCain, despite exit polls favoring Obama, I literally flashed back to the exit poll fiasco of 2004 and to the moment when Florida was called back from

Gore in 2000. Was it possible that the same thing could happen again this year? Despite all the precautions we had taken, could this election veer off course? My palms became sweaty, my heart started to race, and my voice to quake. Fear consumed me. I sort of floated out of my body. In a literal state of disassociation, I called my brother-in-law, a political analyst with access to exit polls, to talk me down. "Johanna", he said, "it's over." "What do you mean?" I asked, seriously, "Is McCain going to win?" "No," he answered with remarkable patience, as if he recognized at that moment just how damaged I was, "Obama has this. This is not 2004." His quiet confidence allowed me to re-enter my body.

A few minutes later, the networks called Pennsylvania for Obama, and an hour after that, Ohio. Florida, Virginia, Colorado, New Mexico, Nevada, even Indiana for God's sake, began to flip blue. A McCain victory started to look like a mathematical impossibility. At 11:00 p.m. the Obama wave finally crashed onto the shore, the planetary "upset" that the astrologist had predicted came to pass, and the crowds in Chicago, Indonesia, Kenya, and Great Britain erupted in joy and relief. I couldn't stop staring at Jesse Jackson's tear-streaked face as he stood alone amid the massive crowd at Grant Park. His look encapsulated to me all of the suffering, grief, elation, doubt, disbelief, agony, triumph, pain and awe that had gone into the making of this moment. Yes, we can, and yes, we did. The ghosts from elections past receded.

The next morning, everyone I passed on the street grinned at each other. As I walked over the

Harvard Square Bridge on my way to work, I paused to admire the sparkling pellets of gold bouncing gingerly along the surface of the Charles River, shimmering against the blue sky. I shut my eyes and swear that I heard a voice say: "You can relax. It's all good now."

In the days that followed, I began to exhale again. I felt flooded with gratitude and affection for every voter who had to overcome his or her own fears and doubts to pull the lever for Obama. I remembered George Packer's prediction in his 2000 book, *Blood of the Liberals,* "with our endless talent for experiment and hope….we will have a more just society as soon as we want one. Throughout American history this desire keeps rising to the surface, often at the unlikeliest moments." I wondered if we had arrived at just such a moment. For scarred election veterans like me, such hopeful and grateful November emotions were a wholly unfamiliar phenomenon.

Recently, John McCain's campaign manager, Steve Schmidt, made the following observation about Barack Obama's victory:

> This was, in my view, the unfinished Bobby Kennedy campaign – the idealism, the passion, the inspiration he gave to people….

I think he got it exactly right. For 40 years, millions of us have been trying, unconsciously, to resurrect Robert Kennedy, or at least to find a candidate who could make us believe again in the possibilities of transformational leadership. "The yearning for Robert F. Kennedy--or somebody like him" Ronald Steel wrote in his 2000 critique *In Love With Night*, "is an open wound in some parts of the country." Well, in Obama, we finally found the "somebody like him." When he won, the haunting ended.

I feel as if a 40-year curse has been lifted. I don't think I'll ever approach an election again as a heartbreak-in-waiting. Whatever the reality of Obama's Presidency, I, along with my fellow travelers, have no more excuses to wallow in our dreams of what might have been. Rather, we have been handed an opportunity that few of us expected to come again in our lifetime: to set our sights on what still might be.

Julene Tripp Weaver

Julene Tripp Weaver has lived in Seattle since 1989. She earned a Bachelor's in creative writing from City University of New York. She earned a Masters in Applied Behavioral Science from the Leadership Institute of Seattle and works in HIV/AIDS Services. Finishing Line Press published her chapbook <u>Case Walking: An AIDS Case Manager Wails her Blues</u>. Garrison Keillor featured a poem from her book on <u>The Writer's Almanac</u>. Her poems have been published in many journals including <u>Main Street Rag</u>, <u>The Healing Muse</u>, <u>Knock</u>, <u>Arabesques Review</u>, <u>Nerve Cowboy</u>, <u>Arnazella</u>, <u>Crab Creek Review</u>, <u>Pilgrimage</u> and <u>Letters to the World Poems</u> from the Wom-Po LISTSERV.

The piece that follows ("Over Here, Over There") appeared previously in *Drash: Northwest Mosaic, 2009/5769*. It is reprinted with their permission.

Over Here, Over There

a spider and I sit
as if nothing is going on
the world is here this corner
my window overlooks a park
a quiet street
here in the western world
I cannot see
destruction's rubble
buildings felled-in-flames
I do not hear the wails of women
in the streets full of gun metal
I pray for redemption from this war

At my corner espresso bar
no suicide bombers explode

my phone rings
my refrigerator hums
my apartment stays warm
I sit and watch
a spider waits its prey
here in the western world
outside my window
I rock in my warm home
I grieve for babies dying
pray for ascension
of my people
so terrifying to me

I turn on the news
wake up   we must   wake up

Stephen Scott Whitaker

Stephen Scott Whitaker is the author of two chapbooks of poetry, and he is a Pushcart Nominee for fiction. His work has been published in dozens of journals and magazines. He is a regular columnist and book reviewer for <u>Delmarva Quarterly</u>, an arts and humanities magazine. He has received an NEA grant for re-writing <u>Romeo and Juliet</u> as a rock musical for high school students.

11/5/08 CNN PROJECTS OBAMA FOR PRESIDENT- 11:00 PM

Because Obama has won today
one must force change

which translates into:

cut out junk food, car pool, save, avoid the drive
through, invest wisely, volunteer, turn off the TV, read
more poetry, read more books. Tell jokes.
If your hair is white
dye it blue. If it is blue dye
it pink. If you drink
too much, learn to like yoga, or poetry,
or painting, or buy art to caress all your days.

If you hate your body change it
and wear the disguises you admire,
they are no more different than boiled bones,
arrowheads, gold chains, black
Wall Street suits.

Because Obama won today
chew patience, for long years
of slow work are paved only one city block at a time.
How long did it take to build the Parthenon?

Because Obama won today
keep it real. Because
Obama won
today
allow yourself
to open up
like the country once was.
Not the geography,
but the spirit.

Because Obama won today eat color,
lean your life, give your heart away.

O Nation, O Heart

Churches, congresses, bars, and circus lights
bridge old deep streets
and lead into the heart of the city,
where a small girl wanders without her mother
humming, and kicking a can down a gutter,
her mother long having left her
lean and long in the shadows.
The girl would thrive on threadbare knuckles,
later become a lawyer,
and associate her mother with tractor trailers.

Chew patience,
Eat color,
Lean your life, give your heart away

The man in the yellow room which
is a room but not
a room as he leans
over his mother dying of cancer,
his mind stretches beyond the exterior of his house
to a time when he could speak.
He doesn't remember
when he lost the nerve
to open his mouth.
Sometime after his wife left him
and his home became
as lonely as a forest,
moonlight filtering down
through maple and oak,
doubt sleeping like a pair of snakes

in the roots of a tree

Cut out junk food, car pool, save, skip the soda, invest
green, volunteer, turn off
the TV, read more
poetry, read more
books. Tell jokes.
If you drink too much, learn
to like zumba, or poetry,
or painting.

Or buy art
from the painter
who sits in her studio
and crushes the same skyline
over and over
because she hasn't awakened
to the conclusion yet,
that she doesn't want to paint, but sing.
Her paintings sell
and they keep her from having to rent out her studio,
though winter was rough.
She lost twenty pounds because she cut back
on everything but electricity, water,
food, and paint,
of course. And then as the white noise
filtered out of mind and body
she realized she was a singer,
but couldn't bare to breathe it,
for to do so would mean destruction.

Wear the disguises you admire,
they are no more different

than boiled bones,
arrowheads, gold chains, black
Wall Street suits, digital camouflage
uniforms.

Chew patience,
eat color,
lean your life, give
your heart away.

The first time he saw her
she was leaning against the counter,
her long blonde hair pooling behind her
on the counter glass,
so it looked like
she was poured there:
in her cut sweater and skirt,
her lips pursed to smoke,
kiss, or swear.
He stared at her every morning
he passed her small kiosk,
the white noise of the Pru
passing through the portal
where she parked every day
since he was hired.
He's talked to her once
or twice. On his tongue
came thrice an invite,
but there was always something,
another customer, a cough, his boss calling his cell,
still she smiled
at him, and remembered
his name

every time he purchased a new pen.
His desk cluttered with shiny ball points,
engraved retirement gifts.

Change life. Give your heart away

Chloe Williams

Chloe Williams lives in upstate NY with her parents and younger brother. She is a senior in high school and runs cross country and track and field. She enjoys reading, camping and skiing. This is her first poem to be published.

The Palin

Once in August, Dems upstaging, Old McCain, ambition raging,
Chose a mate to bring the votes in from the hockey moms out there.
Old John chose Ms. Sarah Palin, sure that they would not be failin'.
In their quest to bring the votes in, they did try to cause a scare:
"Let the Dems in, lose your guns, arms they will not let you bear."
                    Said Ms. Palin: "That's not fair!"

When they talked about Obama, they would make some scary drama.
"Workers work hard for their money, from your hands your cash they'll tear.
He's young and new, he'll tax and spend; we'll end up sorry in the end."
Fear of Muslims they would play on, calling him Hussein they'd dare.
Cutting down Obama-Biden, John and Sarah sought the glare.
                    Said Ms. Palin: "We're the pair!"

When the spotlight's glare did find her, then she got a cruel reminder,
Hockey moms and Joe the Plumber can't afford the suits you wear.
She liked to call herself a maverick, like a pit bull wearing lipstick.
Tina Fey impersonated, copied her with such a flair.
She had the glasses, had the accent, had the voice that was so rare.
                    Said Ms. Palin: "Like my hair?"

Came a Tuesday in November, that the people did remember,
That they wanted change right now, more of the same they could not bear.
Time had come to choose a leader, Sarah hoped no one could beat her.
People came and people voted, showing how much they do care.
Obama-Biden had the vision that the voters chose to share.
                    Said Ms. Palin: "That's not fair!"

Marc Williams

Marc has been writing poetry for the past 31 years. He also composes chamber & vocal music, and practices as a psychotherapist in North Carolina.

The Hang-time of Barack Obama

Tonight, a mile higher than how voters
have before witnessed your messianic
-ally-tinged likeness, we are gathered
as thousands of the faith-full to bestow you
with the crown of *our Father-Saviour,*

even tho younger & blacker than many of us
who saw no such blend of high-talk
& mulatto'd life-clutch coming so soon
in a fresh century, you mantically clearer
than this befuddled, old Republican veteran,
who had any bravery of unmocked politics
tortured out of him forty long years ago—-
you beseeching a new style, milder than substance,
to lead us headlong into our gooier problems
as tho our political salvation will be born from
your steady sorcery of melding our rancor
into alembical balm-calm. We crazily await
your neapolitan presence to juice our fervor
toward the starry transcendence Lincoln offered
to the slaves upon relieving their bondage

& from the poverty known to your own family
of mother, grand-parents & an only son
living around the world until college brought you
to where the poorer of us sulked for jobs
& seethed for cash to forego lives of crime-—
being you are the skinniest Heavenly One

since Jesus took His disciples upon the mountain
& found what dazzles us can also killingly bleed.

Outside this stadium & other lofty podiums,
you are gentler than the barbed, caustic nonsense
of Republican malice castrating Democrats
since Vietnam to rive whites from blacks
& rich from poor—-four years ago at our last
gathering, you reminded us red & blue make purple,
as tho artistry could genially prod our politics
    toward a center naming our real world,

that you have lived the bi-racial tension
of grayer occasions, yet blacker than we whitest
legions of hope in the states lilier than slaves
could ever know, no slavery ever in these states
having come to love you, clamantly calling
for the One who truly knows. Half of you
coaxes the squirming death of our prejudice

to leave the voting booth having prayed
with our fingertips to o'er-leap ancient slavery
thru the whimpering wisdom of spreading
red over white & black in graying our flavours-—
let us carry you upon our hands while passing
your countenance across this huge adoring throng
as the sign of what your words wisely inspire.

Shall we stop yelling for your roiling glory
long enough to hear what in your womanly voice
(echoing a mother's love) says your plans
to save our nation are humbly irresistible,
that you can pellucidly flesh-face a vision:
of slow-swarming equity in cash & taxes,
healing the sick, smartening our children
& cleaning our planetary damage—-how are you
            a mulatto'd elixir of action

to, thru amity's vortex born at last, call
each & all of us here & thruout America
to hang upon what you graciously coax
before the last row-boat before ship-wreck
inevitably comes, such war-wreckage contagious
-ly sprawling still in Iraq, & now after
you visited there, the war has a history
whose end dies in certainter time.

Eight years
finally later, bushed by lies & another youngest
death-trudge, wounded by rotting democracy
's battered Constitution, our favourite grin
-ning idiot soon banished to his Texas pasture—-

we await what of you trims their veteran
down to the babbling anachronism he became
in three debates this autumn, what boils
any less venom than wisdom in your blood,
we no longer so gullible to any politico
's silly slogans, since America is still
soulishly roaming to whittle our gluttony
& crack our bubble-headed, blonder solipsism—-

tell us to sing the harmonies of our sentiments
once you have spoken, softer then louder,
until we feel the trembling tonic of democracy
's lost unity, no half-risk but wholly found.

August 18-20, 2008

Cherise Wyneken

Cherise Wyneken is a freelance writer of prose and poetry. Selections of her work have appeared in a variety of publications, plus two full collections of her poetry, two poetry chapbooks, a memoir, and a novel. You can find more information about Cherise here: http://www.authorsden.com/cherisewyneken

"Re-birth of a Nation" was published online in POETZ, and it is reprinted here with their permission.

Re-birth of a Nation

Dry California hillsides
ripe and round
as a woman's breasts and belly,
ready the ground for
winter green, and my
fair-skinned daughter's womb,
for her black-skinned baby's birth.

Weary American citizens,
suffering from an eight year
drought of good governance,
posed ripe and ready
pens in white-skinned hands
to mark the birth of a
black-skinned president.

Contact Information

Thank you for your purchase of this Bobo Strategy publication.

For more information about the products and services we offer, please contact us.

Bobo Strategy
2506 N Clark #287
Chicago, IL 60614

Website: http://www.BoboStrategy.com

Email: info@BoboStrategy.com

If you liked this book, you might like this one too:

<u>Let Nothing You Dismay</u>, a short novel by Benjamin Shultz

This short novel details the experiences of a self-conscious young man growing up in a small conservative town. The character negotiates normal changes experienced during adolescence against the backdrop of a socially repressive atmosphere.

Publisher: Bobo Strategy (2009)
Details: 90 Pages, Paperback
List Price: $7.95
ISBN: 978-0615285306

Available online and in a store near you.

www.ingramcontent.com/pod-product-compliance
Lightning Source LLC
Chambersburg PA
CBHW031319040426
42443CB00005B/138